Practical Ideas
That Really Work
for Students with ADHD

D0904598

Practical Ideas
That Really Work
for Students with ADHD

Kathleen McConnell

Gail Ryser

Judith Higgins

pro·ed
An International Publisher

8700 Shoal Creek Boulevard
Austin, Texas 78757-6897
800/897-3202 Fax 800/397-7633
Order online at http://www.proedinc.com

© 2000 by PRO-ED, Inc.
8700 Shoal Creek Boulevard
Austin, Texas 78757-6897
800/897-3202 Fax 800/397-7633
Order online at http://www.proedinc.com

Library of Congress Cataloging-in-Publication Data
McConnell, Kathleen.
    Practical ideas that really work for students with ADHD /
Kathleen McConnell, Gail Ryser, Judith Higgins.
        p.   cm.
    Includes bibliographical references (p.   ).
    ISBN 0-89079-837-0 (softcover : alk. paper)
    1. Attention-deficit-disordered children—Education.   2.
Attention-deficit-disordered youth—Education.   I. Ryser, Gail.   II.
Higgins, Judith.   III. Title.
LC4713.2 .M33   2000
371.93—dc21   99-41748
                                                        CIP

Production Director: Alan Grimes
Production Coordinator: Dolly Fisk Jackson
Managing Editor: Chris Olson
Art Director: Thomas Barkley
Designer: Jason Crosier
Print Buyer: Alicia Woods
Preproduction Coordinator: Chris Anne Worsham
Staff Copyeditor: Martin Wilson
Project Editor: Tama Fortner
Publishing Assistant: Jason Morris

Printed in the United States of America

2   3   4   5   6   7   8   9   10   03   02   01   00

Contents

Introduction

We created *Practical Ideas That Really Work for Students with ADHD* for educators who work with students who have attention, impulsivity, or hyperactivity problems that interfere with their ability to learn. The materials are intended for use with students in kindergarten through grade 12 and include two main components:

- *An evaluation form with a rating scale and idea matrix.* The rating scale portion of the evaluation form is a criterion-referenced measure for evaluating behaviors that impact student learning. The items on the scale are specific descriptors that are correlated to the DSM–IV indicators for ADHD. The idea matrix on the evaluation form provides a systematic way of linking the results of the rating scale to interventions. We hope that educators use the matrix as a tool for selecting effective interventions to meet each student's specific needs.

- *A book of practical ideas.* The ideas were written to assist teachers and other professionals in improving students' attending and organization skills and in decreasing their behavior problems related to impulsivity and hyperactivity. The book contains a one-page explanation of each idea, along with reproducible worksheets, examples, illustrations, and tips designed for easy implementation.

The next section of this introduction will describe the development of the rating scale and the ideas, then provide directions for their use.

The Rating Scale

The criterion-referenced rating scale is intended for use by teachers or other professionals to rate students according to the DSM–IV criteria for ADHD. The measure was designed to assist teachers in conducting a careful and thorough assessment of the specific problems to guide the selection of intervention strategies.

The rating scale is divided into the three areas of ADHD defined by the DSM–IV: inattention, hyperactivity, and impulsivity. The measure consists of 54 items: three items for each of the 18 DSM–IV criteria. Educators can use the scale's four-point Likert scale to complete a rating, with a 0 meaning the student never exhibits the behavior and a 3 meaning the student consistently exhibits the behavior to the point where it almost always interferes with the child's ability to function in the learning environment. For each DSM–IV criterion, the range of possible scores is 0 to 9; the higher the score, the more the behavior interferes with learning.

The criterion-referenced measure was field-tested in three school districts in Texas with 84 students identified as having ADHD. The students ranged in age from 6 to 16 years, with 17 females and 67 males. An item analysis was conducted using this sample, and the resulting reliability coefficients were .97 for inattention, .96 for hyperactivity, and .96 for impulsivity. The magnitude of these coefficients strongly suggests that the rating scale possesses little test error and that users can have confidence in its results.

One way of establishing an assessment instrument's validity is to study the performances of different groups of individuals on the instrument. Each group's results should make sense, given what is known about the relationship of the instrument's content to the group. In the case of our rating scale, one would expect that individuals identified as having ADHD would be rated higher by their teachers or other professionals than individuals not so identified. In fact, an instrument whose results did not differentiate between such groups would have no clinical or diagnostic value; it would have no construct validity.

We would expect to find statistically significant differences between individuals identified as having ADHD and those individuals identified as not having them. To test for these differences, three t-tests were conducted (one for each of the three areas of ADHD related to the DSM–IV) with 84 students identified as having ADHD and 22 students with no known disabilities. The Bonferroni procedure was used to control for Type I error and the alpha was set at 0.017. In every case, the group with ADHD was rated higher (i.e., had more difficulty functioning in the learning environment) than the group with no known disabilities. On the inattention total score, the ADHD group had a mean raw score of

58.7 (out of a possible score of 81), with a standard deviation of 17.5. For the no disability group, the mean was 21.7 and the standard deviation was 15.4. On the hyperactivity total score, the ADHD group had a mean raw score of 31.5 (out of a possible score of 54), with a standard deviation of 15.3. For the no disability group, the mean was 9.5 and the standard deviation was 10.4. On the inattention total score, the ADHD group had a mean raw score of 16.7 (out of a possible score of 27), with a standard deviation of 8.1. For the no disability group, the mean was 3.9 and the standard deviation was 16.0. In each comparison, there were statistically significant differences between the mean raw scores of the two groups at the .000 level.

Practical Ideas That Really Work

Teachers and other educators are busy people with many responsibilities. In our discussions with teachers, supervisors, and counselors about the development of this product, they consistently emphasized the need for materials that are practical, easy to implement in the classroom, and not overly time consuming. We appreciated their input and worked hard to meet their criteria as we developed the ideas in this book. In addition, we conducted an extensive review of the literature, so that we stayed focused on effective and widely used ideas. The result is a book with 40 ideas, most with reproducible masters, and all grounded in the research and collective experience of its three authors, as well as the many educators who advised us and shared information with us.

Assessment often provides much useful information to educators about the strengths and deficits of students. However, unless the information gathered during the assessment process impacts instruction, its usefulness for campus-based educators is limited. We designed the idea matrix so that educators can make the direct link between the information provided by the rating scale and instruction in the classroom. We believe that this format stays true to our purpose of presenting information that is practical and useful.

Directions for Using the Materials

The professional (a general education teacher, special education teacher, counselor, or other educator with knowledge of the student) should begin by completing the Evaluation Form for the child who has been identified as ADHD or the child who exhibits problems with inattention, hyperactivity, or impulsivity. As an example, a completed Evaluation Form for a student, Janie, is provided at the end of this section (Figure 1). Space is provided on the front of the form for pertinent information about the student being rated, including name, birth date, age, school, grade, teacher, and subject area. In addition, the dates the student is observed and the amount of time the rater spends with the student can be recorded here. Also included on the front of the form are the DSM–IV criteria for attention-deficit/hyperactivity disorder.

Pages 2 and 3 of the Evaluation Form contain the rating scale. The items are divided into the three sections defined by the DSM–IV criteria: inattention, hyperactivity, and impulsivity. This section provides the instructions for administering and scoring the items. Space is also provided to total the items for each DSM–IV criterion, to check the three problems to target for immediate intervention, and to record the intervention idea and its starting date.

The last page of the Evaluation Form contains the idea matrix. After choosing the three priority problems to target for immediate intervention, the professional should turn to the idea matrix and select an intervention that corresponds to that problem. The professional should write the idea number and the starting date on the space provided on the rating scale.

For example, Janie received the highest ratings in two areas of Inattention (incomplete assignments [9] and unorganized [7]), and one area of Impulsivity (speaks without permission [6]). Her teacher has targeted these three areas and has chosen Ideas 20, 18, and 24 from the idea matrix. Because the area of major concern is incomplete assignments, the teacher will begin with Idea 20 on October 9.

After selecting an idea from the matrix, the teacher should read the one-page explanation, then begin implementing the idea. To aid in implementation, most of the 40 ideas have at least one reproducible form on the page(s) immediately following the explanation. A small icon in the top right-hand corner of the idea page indicates an accompanying form. Some ideas did not lend themselves to a reproducible form, but instead are supported with explanations, suggestions for use, illustrations, tips, resource lists, and boxes of further information. Ideally, the teacher or other professional should evaluate the effectiveness of each intervention. In our example with Janie, this could be accomplished by recording the number of completed assignments during a 3- to 4-week period. If the intervention is successful, the teacher can move onto the second problem and choose a new idea to implement.

Supporting Evidence for the Practical Ideas

The next section provides references that support the practical ideas in the book. These references will provide interested professionals with relevant information should they wish to learn more about the interventions described. The references are grouped by general category.

Using Contracts

DuPaul, G. J., & Stoner, G. (1994). *ADHD in the schools: Assessment and intervention strategies*. New York: The Guilford Press.

Hammill, D. D., & Bartel, N.R. (1995). *Teaching students with learning and behavior problems* (6th ed.). Austin, TX: PRO-ED.

Roberts, M., White, R., & McLaughlin, T. F. (1997). Useful classroom accommodations for teaching children with ADD and ADHD. *B.C. Journal of Special Education, 21*, 71–84.

The Importance of the Classroom Environment

Christian, J. M. (1997). The body as a site of reproduction and resistance: Attention deficit hyperactivity disorder and the classroom. *Interchange, 28*(1), 31–43.

Sulzer-Azaroff, B., & Mayer, G. R. (1991). *Behavior analysis for lasting change*. Fort Worth, TX: Holt, Rinehart, & Winston.

Helping Students Get Organized

Rief, S. F. (1996). Making a difference in the classroom. *The ADHD Report, 4*(2), 9–10.

Stormont-Spurgin, M. (1997). I lost my homework: Strategies for improving organization in students with ADHD. *Intervention in School and Clinic, 32*(5), 270–274.

The Importance of Peer Relationships

DuPaul, G. J., Bankert, C. L., & Ervin, R. A. (1994). Classwide peer tutoring: A school-based academic intervention for ADHD. *The ADHD Report, 2*(4), 4–5.

Gardill, C. M., DuPaul, G. J., & Kyle, K. E. (1996). Classroom strategies for managing students with attention-deficit/hyperactivity disorder. *Intervention in School and Clinic, 32*(2), 89–94. (see also for information on environment)

Sabian, B. (1995). Enhancing self-esteem and social skills in children with ADHD. *The ADHD Report, 3*(5), 8–10.

Using Positive Reinforcement

Abramowitz, A. J., & O'Leary, S. G. (1991). Behavioral interventions for the classroom: Implications for students with ADHD. *School Psychology Review, 20*(2), 220–234.

Ghosh, S., & Chattopadhyay, P. K. (1993). Application of behavior modification techniques in treatment of attention deficit hyperactivity. *Indian Journal of Clinical Psychology, 20*(2), 124–129.

Lock, J. (1996). Developmental considerations in the treatment of school-age boys with ADHD: An example of a group treatment approach. *Journal of the American Academy of Child and Adolescent Psychiatry, 35*(11), 1557–1559.

Edwards, G. (1993). Positive reinforcement and the most favorite supervisor. *The ADHD Report, 5*(1), 9–10.

Solanto, M. V. (1990). The effects of reinforcement and response cost on a delayed response task in children with attention deficit hyperactivity disorder: A research note. *Journal of Child Psychology and Psychiatry and Allied Disciplines, 31*(5), 803–808.

Relaxation/Visualization Techniques

Blanton, J., & Johnson, L. J. (1991). Using computer assisted biofeedback to help children with attention-deficit hyperactivity disorder to gain self-control. *Journal of Special Education Technology, 11*(1), 49–56.

Braswell, L., & Bloomquist, M. L. (1991). *Cognitive-behavioral therapy with ADHD children.* New York: The Guilford Press.

Calhoun, G., Fees, C. K., & Bolton, J. A. (1994). Attention-deficit hyperactivity disorder: Alternatives for psychotherapy? [Special Issue]. *Perceptual and Motor Skills, 79*(1, Pt. 2).

Friedman, R. J., & Doyal, G. T. (1992). *Management of children and adolescents with attention deficit-hyperactivity disorder* (3rd ed.). Austin, TX: PRO-ED.

Wood, J. W., & Frith, G. H. (1984). Drug therapy? Let's take a closer look. *Academic Therapy, 20*(2) 149–157.

Teaching Students to Self-Monitor

Barkley, R. A., Copeland, A., & Sivage, C. (1980). A self-control classroom for hyperactive children. *Journal of Autism and Developmental Disorders, 10,* 75–89.

Edwards, L. (1995). Effectiveness of self-management on attentional behavior and reading comprehension for children with attention deficit disorder. *Child and Family Behavior Therapy, 17*(2), 1–17.

Harris, K. R. (1986). Self-monitoring of attentional behavior versus self-monitoring of productivity: Effects on on-task behavior and academic response rate among learning disabled children. *Journal of Applied Behavior Analysis, 19*(4), 417–423.

Hoff, K. E., & DuPaul, G. J. (1998). Reducing disruptive behavior in general education classrooms: The use of self-management strategies. *School Psychology Review, 27*(2), 290–303.

Mathes, M. Y., & Bender, W. N. (1997). The effects of self-monitoring on children with attention-deficit/hyperactivity disorder who are receiving pharmacological interventions. *Remedial and Special Education, 18*(2), 121–128.

Snider, V. E. (1987). Professional dialogue: Self monitoring of attention. A response to Hallahan and Lloyd. *Learning Disability Quarterly, 10*(2), 157–159.

Using Signals and Cues with Students

Christie, D. J., Hiss, M., & Lozanoff, B. (1984). Modification of inattentive classroom behavior: Hyperactive children's use of self-recording with teacher guidance. *Behavior Modification, 8*(3), 391–406.

Fraser, C., Belzner, R., & Conte, R. (1992). Attention deficit hyperactivity disorder and self-control: A single case study of the use of a timing device in the development of self-monitoring. *School Psychology International, 13*(4), 339–345.

Becker, L. D. (1999). Non-audible reminder and training watch for persons with ADHD. *The ADHD Report, 7*(1), 7–8.

Developing and Implementing Token Systems

Barkley, R. A. (1996). 18 ways to make token systems more effective for ADHD children and teens. *The ADHD Report, 4*(4), 1–5.

Luiselli, J. K. (1994). A multicomponent classroom intervention for independent academic productivity. *The ADHD Report, 2*(5), 5–7.

Acknowledgments

There are a number of individuals we would like to thank for their help in preparing these materials. Special thanks go to Chris Anne Worsham, whose creativity, dedication, and skills helped make this work a reality. Chris Anne is a pleasure to work with and, throughout this process, gave us hours of her time and expertise.

We are also grateful to Paula Rogers and Michele Harmon, directors of Special Education, and to teachers from all over Texas. They took time from their busy schedules to provide us with data for our reliability and validity studies of the rating scale. Finally, we also thank Dr. Jim Patton, executive editor at PRO-ED, for his encouragement and critical eye. He helped fine-tune this product and kept us on track as we developed something we hope will benefit students and teachers.

Practical Ideas
That Really Work
for Students with ADHD

Kathleen McConnell
Gail Ryser
Judith Higgins

Evaluation Form

Name Janie Sanford

Birth Date 3-14-88   Age 12

School Washington Middle School   Grade 7

Rater teacher—Mr. Watson

Subject Area Social Studies

Dates Student Observed: From 8-9-00 To 10-2-00

Amount of Time Spent with Student:

Per Day 45 min.   Per Week

DSM-IV Diagnostic Criteria for Attention-Deficit/Hyperactivity Disorder

A. Either (1) or (2):

(1) six (or more) of the following symptoms of **inattention** have persisted for at least 6 months to a degree that is maladaptive and inconsistent with developmental level:

Inattention

(a) often fails to give close attention to details or makes careless mistakes in schoolwork, work, or other activities

(b) often has difficulty sustaining attention in tasks or play activities

(c) often does not seem to listen when spoken to directly

(d) often does not follow through on instructions and fails to finish schoolwork, chores, or duties in the workplace (not due to oppositional behavior or failure to understand instructions)

(e) often has difficulty organizing tasks and activities

(f) often avoids, dislikes, or is reluctant to engage in tasks that require sustained mental effort (such as schoolwork or homework)

(g) often loses things necessary for tasks or activities (e.g., toys, school assignments, pencils, books, or tools)

(h) is often easily distracted by extraneous stimuli

(i) is often forgetful in daily activities

(2) six (or more) of the following symptoms of **hyperactivity-impulsivity** have persisted for at least 6 months to a degree that is maladaptive and inconsistent with developmental level:

Hyperactivity

(a) often fidgets with hands or feet or squirms in seat

(b) often leaves seat in classroom or in other situations in which remaining seated is expected

(c) often runs about or climbs excessively in situations in which it is inappropriate (in adolescents or adults, may be limited to subjective feelings of restlessness)

(d) often has difficulty playing or engaging in leisure activities quietly

(e) is often "on the go" or often acts as if "driven by a motor"

(f) often talks excessively

Impulsivity

(g) often blurts out answers before questions have been completed

(h) often has difficulty awaiting turn

(i) often interrupts or intrudes on others (e.g., butts into conversations or games)

Note. From the *Diagnostic and Statistical Manual of Mental Disorders, Fourth Edition,* 1994, Washington, DC: American Psychiatric Association. Copyright 1994 by American Psychiatric Association. Reprinted with permission.

Additional copies of this form (#9167) may be purchased from PRO-ED, 8700 Shoal Creek Blvd., Austin, TX 78757-6897
512/451-3246, Fax 512/451-8542

Figure 1. Sample Evaluation Form, filled out for Janie.

Rating Scale

DIRECTIONS

❶ Use the following scale to circle the appropriate number:

0 = Never exhibits the behavior.

1 = Rarely exhibits the behavior so it almost never interferes with the child's ability to function in the learning environment.

2 = Sometimes exhibits the behavior so at times it interferes with the child's ability to function in the learning environment.

3 = Consistently exhibits the behavior to the point where it almost always interferes with the child's ability to function in the learning environment.

❷ Total the ratings and record in the Total box.

❸ Put a check in the Immediate Intervention column by the top three problems. (Give special consideration to those items with totals ≥ 6.)

❹ Select up to three solutions from the matrix for each problem, and write the number and start date for each in the blanks provided in the last column.

BEHAVIOR	RATING	TOTAL	IMMEDIATE INTERVENTION	SOLUTIONS; START DATE

Inattention

Never / Rarely / Sometimes / Consistently

Makes careless mistakes

1 Turns in sloppy work. — 0 (1) 2 3

2 Gets low grades as a result of carelessness. — 0 (1) 2 3

3 Fails to give close attention to schoolwork. — 0 1 (2) 3

TOTAL: 4 — ○

Doesn't stay focused

1 Frequently shifts the focus of the conversation. — 0 (1) 2 3

2 Has difficulty sticking with a task through completion. — 0 1 (2) 3

3 Changes to a new activity before completing the previous activity. — 0 1 (2) 3

TOTAL: 5 — ○

Doesn't listen

1 Asks the teacher to repeat instructions. — 0 (1) 2 3

2 Has difficulty following multiple step directions. — 0 (1) 2 3

3 Seems to be daydreaming when spoken to directly. — 0 1 (2) 3

TOTAL: 4 — ○

Incomplete assignments

1 Daydreams instead of working on in-class assignments, even though he or she understands instructions. — 0 1 2 (3)

2 Completes only portions of assignments. — 0 1 2 (3)

3 Has difficulty following through on teacher requests. — 0 1 2 (3)

TOTAL: 9 — ✓ — 20   10-9-00

Unorganized

1 Has difficulty keeping track of assignments. — 0 1 (2) 3

2 Is a poor planner. — 0 1 2 (3)

3 Has an unorganized and messy notebook. — 0 1 (2) 3

TOTAL: 7 — ✓ — 18   10-30-00 / 23   10-30-00

Lacks sustained attention

1 Is off-task. — 0 1 (2) 3

2 Has difficulty concentrating. — 0 (1) 2 3

3 Has difficulty completing long-term projects. — 0 1 (2) 3

TOTAL: 5 — ○

Loses supplies

1 Loses homework assignments. — 0 1 (2) 3

2 Loses school supplies. — 0 1 (2) 3

3 Damages tools (e.g., calculator) necessary for completing schoolwork as a result of carelessness. — 0 (1) 2 3

TOTAL: 5 — ○

Easily distracted

1 Attends to what is happening outside the classroom instead of staying on-task. — 0 (1) 2 3

2 Has trouble concentrating. — 0 1 (2) 3

3 Is easily distracted. — 0 1 (2) 3

TOTAL: 5 — ○

Forgetful

1 Forgets to take important papers home or give them to parents. — 0 1 (2) 3

2 Forgets to study for a test or quiz. — 0 (1) 2 3

3 Misplaces pencils, pens, and papers while in class. — 0 1 (2) 3

TOTAL: 5 — ○

Figure 1. Continued.

BEHAVIOR	RATING				TOTAL	IMMEDIATE INTERVENTION	SOLUTIONS; START DATE
	Never	Rarely	Sometimes	Consistently			

Hyperactivity

Fidgets, wiggles

1 Has difficulty sitting still in desk. — 0 (1) 2 3
2 Drums fingers or taps pencil or other objects. — 0 1 (2) 3   **[4]** ○ ___ ___
3 Wiggles or squirms excessively. — 0 (1) 2 3

Out of seat

1 Leaves seat without permission. — 0 (1) 2 3
2 Gets up to wander around the room. — 0 (1) 2 3   **[2]** ○ ___ ___
3 Has difficulty staying seated during presentations or special events. — (0) 1 2 3

Excessive movement

1 Is restless. — 0 (1) 2 3
2 Jumps or climbs on furniture. — (0) 1 2 3   **[1]** ○ ___ ___
3 Runs in the hallways when passing from class to class. — (0) 1 2 3

Difficulty with quiet activities

1 Shifts from one activity to another during free time. — 0 (1) 2 3
2 Has difficulty playing quietly. — (0) 1 2 3   **[2]** ○ ___ ___
3 Is easily excited. — 0 (1) 2 3

Never stops moving

1 Is "on-the-go." — 0 (1) 2 3
2 Engages in physically dangerous activities. — (0) 1 2 3   **[2]** ○ ___ ___
3 Has trouble slowing down or relaxing. — 0 (1) 2 3

Talks excessively

1 Makes excessive noise during quiet activities. — 0 (1) 2 3
2 Talks too much. — 0 1 (2) 3   **[4]** ○ ___ ___
3 Dominates conversations so that others cannot "get a word in edgewise." — 0 (1) 2 3

Impulsivity

Speaks without permission

1 Blurts out answers. — 0 1 (2) 3
2 Has difficulty waiting for directions before proceeding. — 0 1 (2) 3   **[6]** ✓ 24 11-6-00
3 Has trouble waiting for teachers or others to complete their question before responding. — 0 1 (2) 3

Can't wait for turn

1 Has difficulty taking turns when playing games. — 0 (1) 2 3
2 Makes comments out of turn. — 0 1 (2) 3   **[4]** ○ ___ ___
3 Fails to wait for his or her turn. — 0 (1) 2 3

Interrupts others; grabs materials

1 Interrupts others in casual conversation. — 0 (1) 2 3
2 Intrudes on others in social situations. — 0 (1) 2 3   **[2]** ○ ___ ___
3 Grabs objects from others. — (0) 1 2 3

Figure 1. Continued.

Ideas Matrix

Ideas	Makes Careless Mistakes	Doesn't Stay Focused	Doesn't Listen	Incomplete Assignments	Unorganized	Lacks Sustained Attention	Loses Supplies	Easily Distracted	Forgetful	Fidgets, Wiggles	Out of Seat	Excessive Movement	Quiet Activities	Never Stops Moving	Talks Excessively	Speaks Without Permission	Can't Wait for Turn	Interrupts and Grabs
	Inattention									**Hyperactivity**						**Impulsivity**		
1 Graphic Organizers	•			•	•													
2 Story Reviews	•	•		•	•													
3 Problem Solvers	•	•	•	•	•	•			•									
4 Compare/Contrast	•			•	•													
5 Mnemonics	•	•	•		•	•												
6 Boundaries	•	•		•		•		•										
7 Self-Checklist	•			•				•	•									
8 Finished Sample			•	•	•	•												
9 Neatness Points	•	•			•													
10 Random Checks		•				•		•		•	•		•	•	•			
11 Headphones		•				•		•										
12 Nonverbal Cues		•	•	•		•		•										
13 Readers	•		•	•		•		•										
14 Picture This		•	•	•		•		•										
15 On-Task Awareness		•				•		•										
16 Victim Cards		•	•		•		•									•	•	
17 Teacher Talk Time		•	•			•		•			•					•	•	
18 Contract	•	•		•	⊙	•				•	•	•				•	•	•
19 Bragging Buddies		•		⊙														
20 Homework Assignments		•		⊙	•	•			•									
21 Questioning Techniques		•	•			•		•								•	•	
22 Visual Contracts					•							•				•		•
23 Organize Materials				⊙			•											
24 Countoons				•								•				⊙	•	•
25 Reminders				•	•	•	•	•	•									
26 Structured Format				•	•		•		•									
27 Get Out Free						•		•			•							
28 Team Checkers		•	•	•		•			•									
29 Relaxation										•		•	•	•	•			
30 Visualization						•		•					•				•	•
31 Quiet Corner										•	•	•	•	•	•	•	•	•
32 Get Physical										•	•	•	•	•				
33 Visual Warning										•	•				•	•		•
34 Modify Distracters										•					•			
35 Three Bs															•		•	•
36 Audiotapes														•	•	•		
37 Nonverbal Signals															•	•	•	
38 Point and Clap										•			•		•	•	•	•
39 Behavior Forms	•	•	•	•	•	•	•	•	•	•		•	•	•	•	•	•	•
40 Positive Reinforcement	•	•	•	•	•			•	•		•	•	•	•	•	•		•

Figure 1. Continued.

Idea 1
Use Basic Graphic Organizers

All students can benefit from graphic organizers. By starting with basic graphic designs and teaching students how they work, teachers can provide a framework upon which students can expand as they progress through school. Once students know the basics, teachers can begin to introduce specialized graphic organizers for individual subjects or types of assignments. Some of the most common graphic organizers are presented here, along with simple directions for their use.

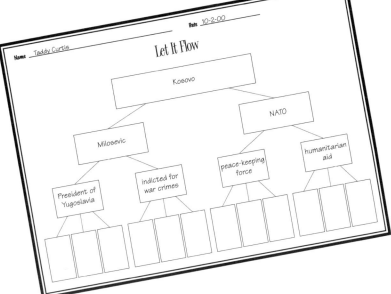

Directions for Forms

Table It

To organize information by category, topic, group, or characteristic, write those headings across the top row. In the first column, list the specific names or items being studied. Then fill in the boxes with the corresponding information.

Let It Flow

As you teach students a hierarchy in any content area, model the use of this structure by putting the influential or powerful item (e.g., person, position, or concept) in the large box at the top. Fill in the lower level boxes with subtopics and supporting information, becoming more specific and isolated as you progress down the hierarchy.

Take Note

Teach students to use a 3-column format to take notes from their reading or from a direct instruction lesson. In the first column, have students write a word, person's name, or concept. In the second column, students should write the definition, explanation, or main points for the word written in the first column. Finally, in the third column, students should write some key words or a mnemonic, or draw a picture to help them remember. To study for a test, students can fold their papers so that only one column at a time is visible. They should practice saying or writing the information from the other columns.

Table It

★	_____	_____	_____
_____			
_____			
_____			

Idea 1

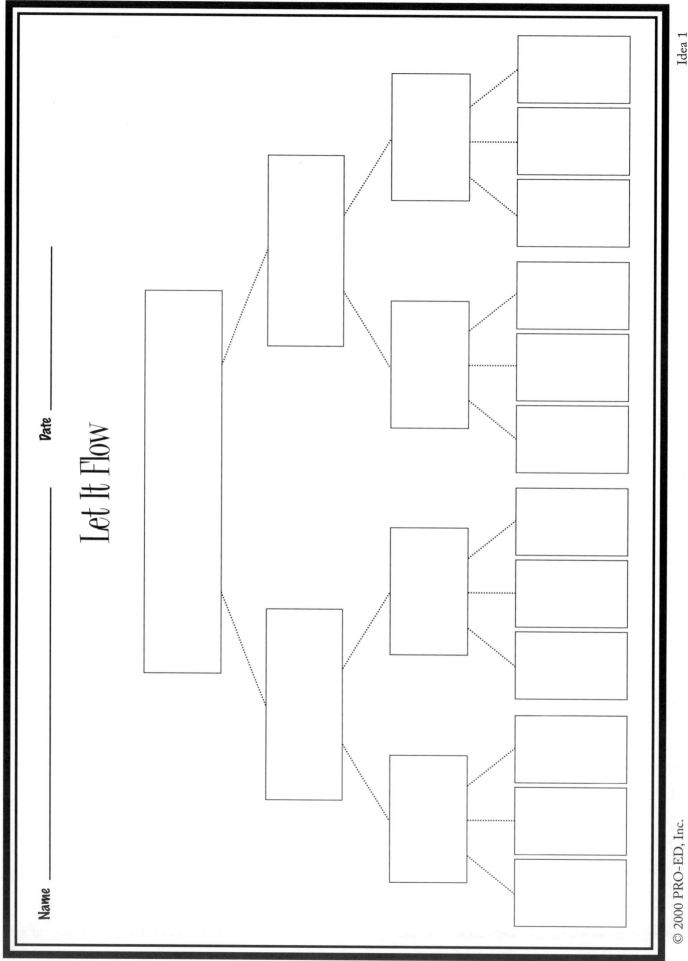

Name

Date

Let It Flow

Take Note

Concept, Name, or Word	Main Points, Definition, or Explanation	Key Words, Mnemonic, or Picture
●	●	●
●	●	●
●	●	●
●	●	●
●	●	●
●	●	●

Idea 1

Idea 2
Use Story Review Graphic Organizers

All students can learn to use organizers and structures that assist them with sequencing and comprehension when they read, watch videos, or listen to lectures. Several graphic organizers are provided in this section that will help students:

- Understand what they read and hear.
- Keep the information organized.
- Study for quizzes and tests.

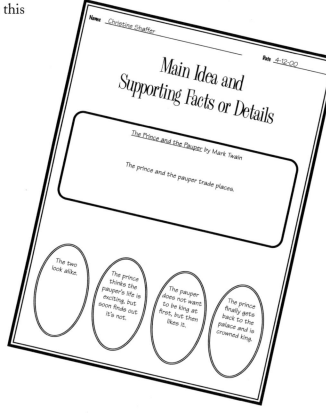

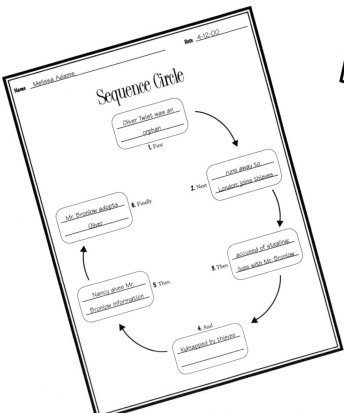

Directions for Forms

Main Idea and Supporting Facts or Details

Teach students to use this form to record the main idea of a content area passage, story, or introduction to a lecture, and then to write down supporting facts as they hear them. Demonstrate by reading a passage aloud and writing the main ideas and details on an overhead of this form. Stop before and after filling in each section to ask students for ideas, then to double-check their comprehension.

Story Chart

Two versions of this form are provided, one for younger students and one for older students. To demonstrate the use of this form, reproduce it on an overhead or enlarge it onto a chart tablet page. Read a short passage aloud, pausing to write an important event in each box. Next time, have students write events on their own papers, and then compare them to your completed form. Soon they should be able to fill in the form independently as they read or listen.

Sequence Circle

To help students retell a story or the sequence of events in a passage, teach them to write those events on the Sequence Circle. This is a quick and easy tool that helps students see the sequence of events, the relationships among occurrences, and the causes and effects.

Main Idea and
Supporting Facts or Details

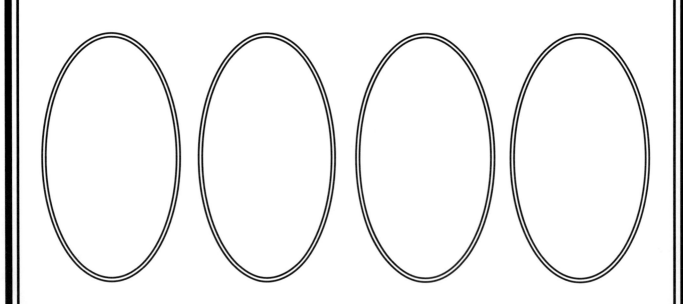

Story Chart

Fill in the events of the story as they happen.

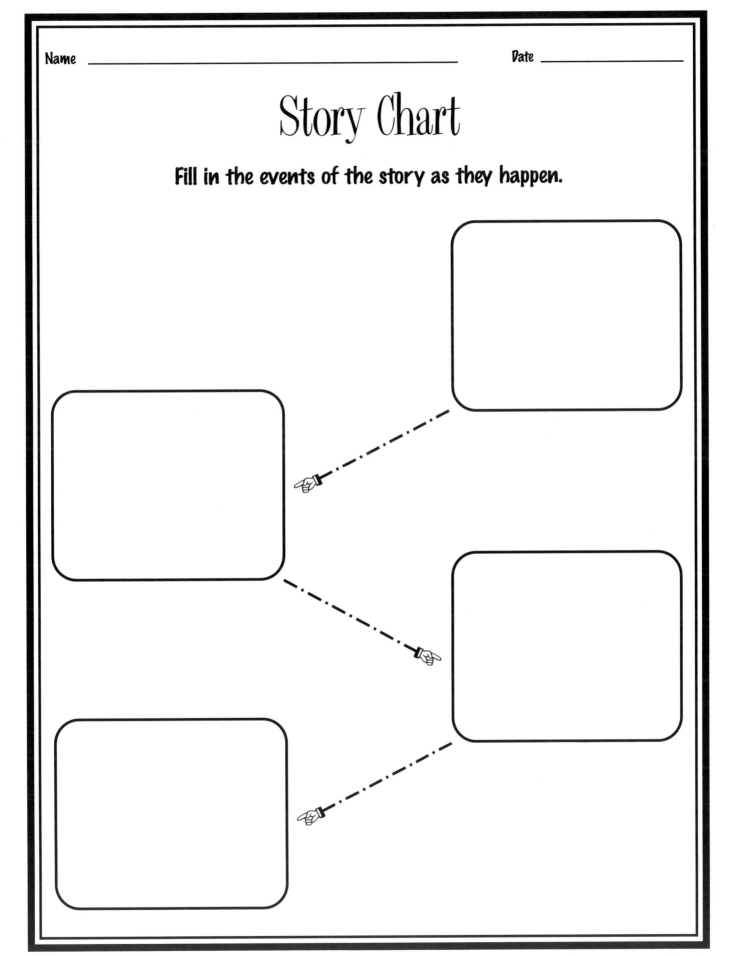

Story Chart

Fill in the events of the story as they happen.

18

Sequence Circle

1. First

2. Next

3. Then

4. And

5. Then

6. Finally

Idea 2

Idea 3
Use Problem-Solver Graphic Organizers

Form Provided

Some strategies, such as graphic organizers, can help **all students** take a step-by-step approach to solving problems and memorizing information. These organizers can be used to solve math problems, conduct science experiments, arrange historical events in chronological order, or complete any sequence of important facts.

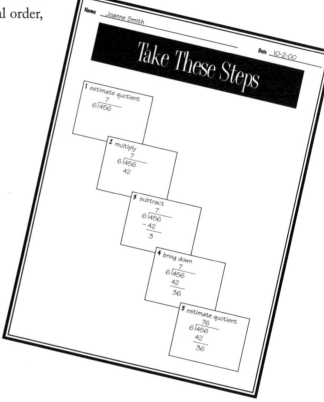

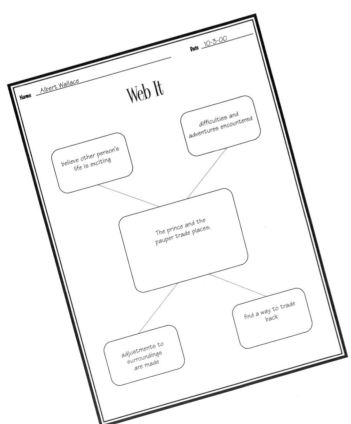

Directions for Forms

Take These Steps

Take These Steps is a simple form to help students organize information. Have students write information in the boxes, and then use the form as a study guide by retracing the steps. This form is great for math problems and science experiments. Two versions are provided, one for younger students and one for older students.

Chart It

This simple chart can be used by students to help them organize information for many different subject areas. Possible heading examples include the following:

- **Science**
  Observation   Hypothesis   Experiment   Results   Conclusion

- **Math** *(Use headings to represent numbers and signs in an equation.)*
  _____   +   _____   =   _____

- **Language Arts**
  Setting   Characters   Main Event   Theme   Your Reaction

Web It

Many teachers use webs for instruction, to introduce topics, as a prewriting tool, to improve comprehension, and to explain relationships. Two webs are provided, one for younger students and one for older students.

Take These Steps

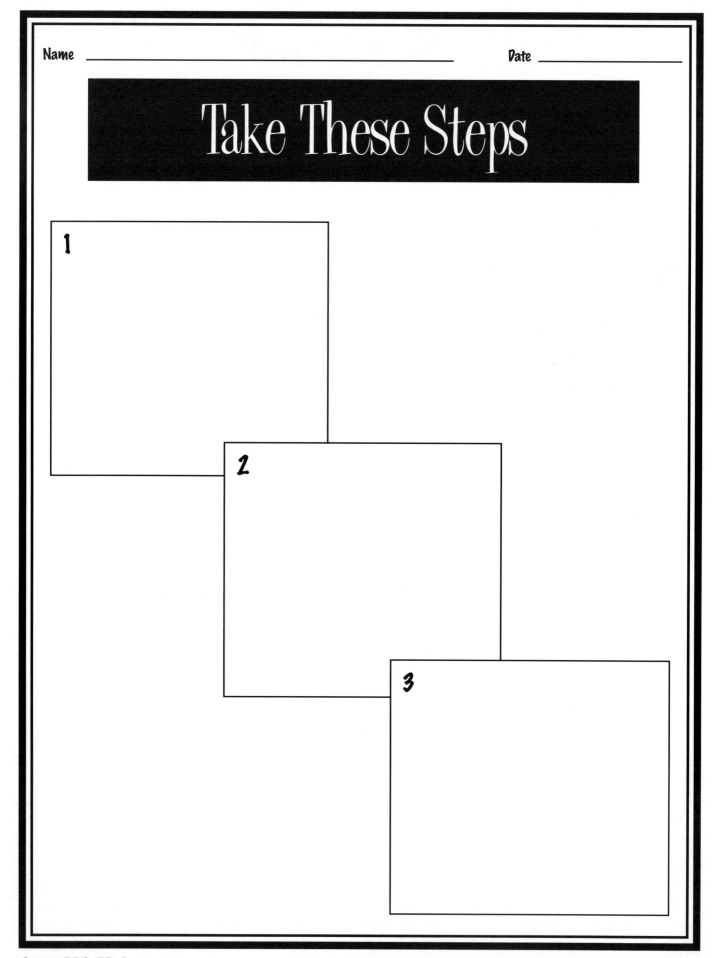

1

2

3

Idea 3

Take These Steps

1

2

3

4

5

Name _____ Date _____

Chart It

Idea 3

Web It

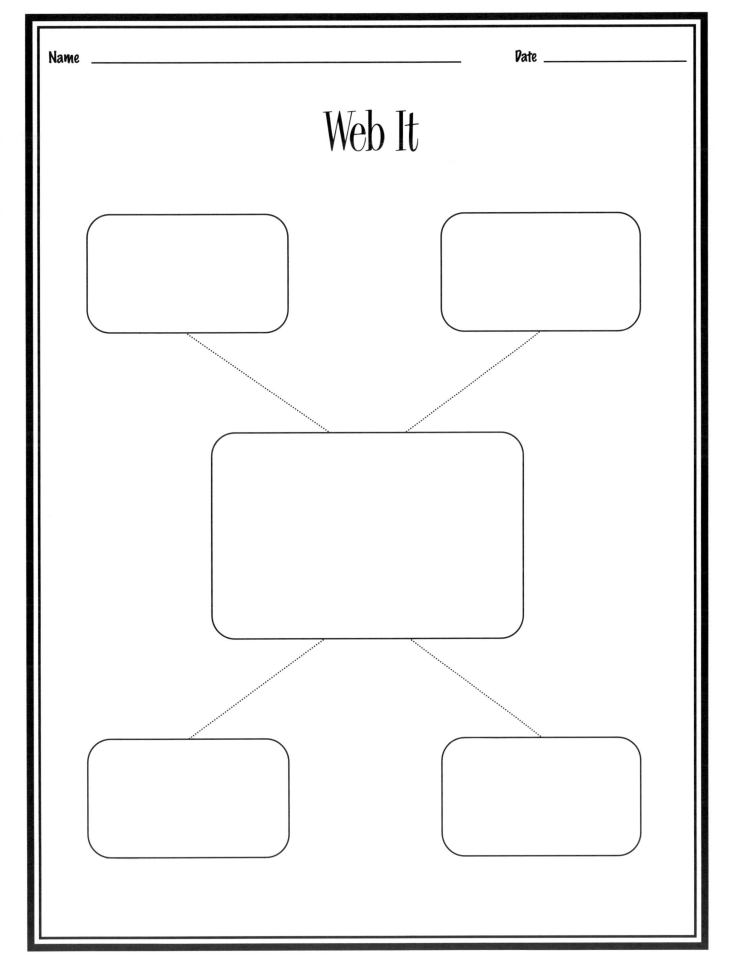

Idea 3

Web It

Idea 3

Idea 4
Use Compare and Contrast Graphic Organizers

All students benefit from learning the skills of comparing and contrasting. These skills help students as they categorize and eventually master concepts by determining whether items and ideas are the same or different. The three graphic organizers in this section should make it easier for students to compare things that are alike and to contrast things that are different.

Name Jason Morris

Date 4-21-00

Same/Different

1
verb

2
noun

Different

Same

Different

expresses an act

words

names something

usually the predicate

part of a sentence

usually the subject

Name Jorge Rodriquez

Date 4-21-00

Venn Diagram

Different

rhombus

• two pairs of parallel sides

• all 4 sides are same length

Same

• polygon

• angles sum to 360°

• 4 sided

Different

trapezoid

• one pair parallel sides

• one pair of sides same length

Directions for Forms

Same/Different

The Same/Different form is useful for students as th... entiate and compare two ideas, obj... on. Instruct students to p... at the top; then to list cha... are different in the left col... second thing in the right c... they have in common in th... for discussion, writing, and s...

Venn Diagram

Venn diagrams are commonly ... taught how to fill in the diagra... Diagram can be used in the sam... The boundaries and visual repre... who can fit their writing into the... staying on the regular lines of not...

Compare and Contrast

The Compare and Contrast form is designed specifically for use with books or videos. Students should write the names of the two books or videos on the lines on the sides of the paper, then fill in the required information to explain how the setting, characters, events or problems, and ending or theme are related.

Same/Different

1	2
_____	_____

Different	Same	Different

Idea 4

Venn Diagram

Different

Same

Different

Name _____

Date _____

Compare and Contrast

1st Story or Book

Title _____

_____

_____

_____

2nd Story or Book

Title _____

_____

_____

_____

Setting

Characters

Events/Problems

Ending/Theme

Idea 5
Teach a Self-Check Strategy by Using a Mnemonic

For students of all ages, here's a simple and commonly used acronym that can be adapted or expanded to help students check their work for neatness—"STOP." You can post this, then teach it to your students through recitation, repetition, and practice. Use the form as a cover sheet that students fill out and attach on top of each assignment. Also provided is a math problem-solving mnemonic, "FRED." It's fun to think of new strategies, so help your students generate mnemonics that work for them.

Name __Luke Shepherd__
Date __11-14-00__

S T O P

Check your work for:

Spelling

Title

OK Looking

Punctuation

Name __Martha Riser__
Date __11-14-00__

F R E D

To do the problem:

Find the Question

Read

Eliminate and Estimate

Do the Problem

S T O P

Check your work for:

Spelling ☐

Title ☐

OK Looking ☐

Punctuation ☐

Idea 5

S T O P

Check your work for:

Sentence Structure ☐

Thesis Statement ☐

Overall Appearance ☐

Punctuation ☐

Idea 5

F R E D

To do the problem:

Find the Question   ☐

Read   ☐

Eliminate and Estimate   ☐

Do the Problem   ☐

Idea 5

Idea 6
Put Boundaries on Worksheets and Assignment Papers

For younger students, provide boundaries for their answers to questions. You can use boxes, columns, dotted lines, or folds in the paper. Some examples are provided that you can use for almost any subject, including math problems.

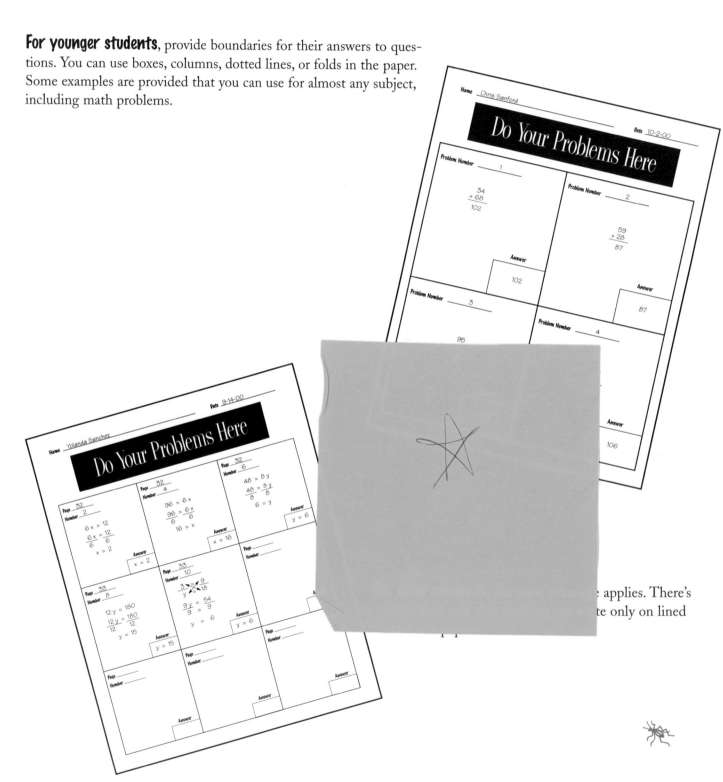

...e applies. There's
...te only on lined

Do Your Problems Here

Problem Number _____

Answer

Problem Number _____

Answer

Problem Number _____

Answer

Problem Number _____

Answer

Idea 6

Do Your Problems Here

Page _____ Number _____	Page _____ Number _____	Page _____ Number _____
Answer	Answer	Answer
Page _____ Number _____	Page _____ Number _____	Page _____ Number _____
Answer	Answer	Answer
Page _____ Number _____	Page _____ Number _____	Page _____ Number _____
Answer	Answer	Answer

Idea 6

Idea 7
Create a Self-Checklist

For younger students, use pictures or symbols. Put Velcro blocks on each square and attach picture symbols indicating steps and directions. Teach students to move each Velcro block from left to right after completing the activity or task it represents. After finishing a lesson or task, replace the picture symbols with those appropriate for the next lesson.

✔ If you laminate this form, it will travel better from class to class and last longer.

For older students, use written words and a checklist format. Don't make the checklist too long, or students won't be able to keep track of things. Four or five items at a time are probably enough.

Name _Stacy Wilson_   **Date** _5-16-00_

Did you do it?

Put a check in the box after you complete each task.

☑

1 Bring all your materials to class.   ☑

2 Listen carefully to the lesson.   ☑

3 Write the assignment down in your assignment notebook.   ☐

4 Complete the assignment.   ☐

5 Turn in your assignment on time.

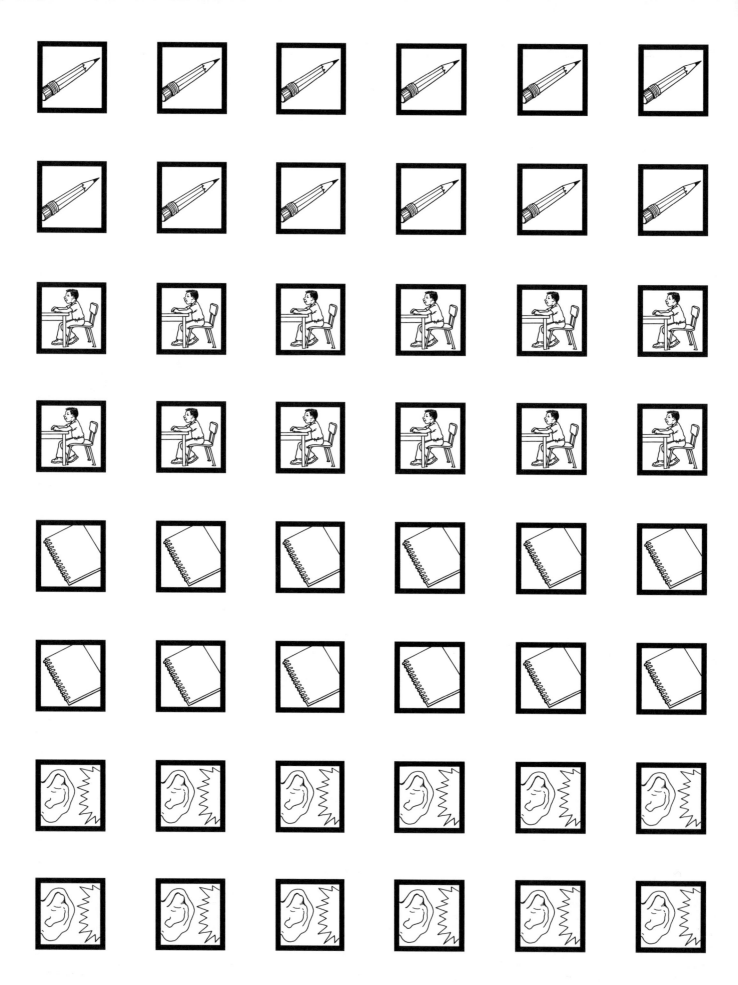

Check It Off

41

Idea 7

Did you do it?

Put a check in the box after you complete each task.

1 _____ ☐

2 _____ ☐

3 _____ ☐

4 _____ ☐

5 _____ ☐

Idea 7

Idea 8
Provide a Finished Sample of the Assignment

For younger students, always do at least one problem or answer at least one question. Use the overhead or board to demonstrate.

For older students, photocopy a finished product that you have saved from an earlier year or from another class. Remove the name of the student who did the assignment. Then make an overhead and/or photocopies of the example. Show the example as you explain what you want, or make copies for each student so that they see how you want things done. Use concrete examples of each part of the assignment that contributes to the overall grade.

Idea 9
Give Bonus Points, Tickets, or Other Rewards for Neatness
(Regardless of Right or Wrong Answers)

For younger students, use coupons that let them know you appreciate their neat work. Be specific about what it is they have to do to earn a coupon. After students receive coupons, have each one write his or her name on the back of it. Put the coupons in a large plastic jar. At the end of the day, reach into the jar and pick one. The student whose name is drawn gets a goodie (special pencil, new folder, big new eraser, extra computer time, etc.).

For older students, the same idea works. Just change the reward so that it is something they value (e.g., skipping a homework assignment or two extra points added on to their test average).

Neat-O

Your work is sooooo neat!

Good Job

Neat-O

Your work is sooooo neat!

Good Job

Neat-O

Your work is sooooo neat!

Good Job

Neat-O

Your work is sooooo neat!

Good Job

Neat-O

Your work is sooooo neat!

Good Job

Neat-O

Your work is sooooo neat!

Good Job

Neatness Counts

This coupon recognizes your:

- ❑ Neat Handwriting
- ❑ Heading
- ❑ Complete Assignment
- ❑ Editing

Neatness Counts

This coupon recognizes your:

- ❑ Neat Handwriting
- ❑ Heading
- ❑ Complete Assignment
- ❑ Editing

Neatness Counts

This coupon recognizes your:

- ❑ Neat Handwriting
- ❑ Heading
- ❑ Complete Assignment
- ❑ Editing

Neatness Counts

This coupon recognizes your:

- ❑ Neat Handwriting
- ❑ Heading
- ❑ Complete Assignment
- ❑ Editing

Neatness Counts

This coupon recognizes your:

- ❑ Neat Handwriting
- ❑ Heading
- ❑ Complete Assignment
- ❑ Editing

Neatness Counts

This coupon recognizes your:

- ❑ Neat Handwriting
- ❑ Heading
- ❑ Complete Assignment
- ❑ Editing

Idea 9

Idea 10
Use Random Checks To Monitor Attending

For younger students, use a timer. Set the timer, but don't tell your students when it's going to go off. (You can face the timer toward a wall or window.) Everyone who is attending when the timer goes off gets a check mark. Each check mark earns two minutes of extra recess, a coupon for the class store, a raffle ticket, and so on.

✔ You can do random checks several different ways, but the principle is the same: to monitor and reinforce students' attention to task at regular but unpredictable intervals.

For older students, create and use an audiotape that lasts for the class period. At random intervals record a sound such as a beep, chime, or gentle buzz. When the noise goes off, each student should ask himself or herself, "Am I working?" If the answer is yes, the student earns a class participation point. Points can be added to the classwork average or participation grade. The points can also be used as part of a contract system.

Am I Working?

Yes   No

Yes   No

Yes   No

Yes   No

Yes   No

Yes   No

Yes   No

Yes   No

Yes   No

Yes   No

Yes   No

Am I Working?

Yes	No
☐	☐
☐	☐
☐	☐
☐	☐
☐	☐
☐	☐
☐	☐
☐	☐
☐	☐
☐	☐
☐	☐
☐	☐
☐	☐

Idea 10

Idea 11
Provide Headphones or Earplugs

For younger students, use large foam earplugs. These earplugs usually cost less than a dollar and are great tools for shutting out sounds. Each student can keep his or her earplugs in a plastic zipper baggie with his or her name on it and can use them during quiet reading or seatwork times.

Older students can use headphones. The headphones can be used just to screen out noise, or they can be attached to a radio or CD/tape player that plays soothing, quiet music. Many students respond well to classical music with no lyrics.

Ordering Information for Earplugs and Headphones

Howard Leight Industries
7828 Waterville Road
San Diego, CA 92173
800/543-0121
www.howardleight.com/about.html

Precision Laboratories, Inc.
800/711-7317
www.precisionweb.com/mail/index.html

Mack's Earplugs
McKeon Products, Inc.
P.O. Box 69009
Pleasant Ridge, MI 48069-0009
248/548-7560
www.imall.com/stores/mack/mack3.html
Mack's Earplugs can be ordered by your pharmacy.

Idea 12
Use Nonverbal Cues

All students can benefit from nonverbal reminders, which also have the advantage of not interrupting instruction. One way to do this is to meet privately with the student and agree on an individualized gesture that will be used only for him or her. The gesture could be a tap on the shoulder, a finger to the lips (like a "shhhh" sign, or a raised hand or finger). When the student sees the teacher use the gesture, he or she should get back to work without talking.

Back to Work

Open Your Book

Another Idea

A more concrete way to signal students involves the use of small cue cards with simple messages. As the teacher moves around the room, he or she can cue a student who is off-task by simply placing a card on the student's desk. We suggest copying the card on brightly colored stock paper and laminating it before use, so that it is visible and reusable. For students who cannot read well, use cards that have both words and pictures or symbols on them.

Time to Work

Get Started

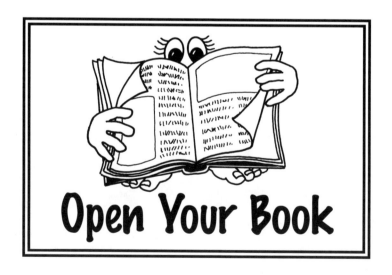

Open Your Book

Back to Work	Get Busy
Pay Attention	Get Started
Eyes On the Teacher	1 · 2 · 3 Go
Open Your Book	Time to Begin

53

Idea 12

Idea 13
Find Readers for Students Who Learn Better by Listening

When students cannot read well or do not focus on tasks, it decreases their understanding. After a while, they may tune out and stop trying. They may even become behavior problems in order to get out of the assignment or the class.

All students can benefit when material is presented orally as well as visually. You can provide help for students by reading aloud to them or letting them work with partners or in a group. But it's nice to have a library of audiotapes available when you or other adults are busy.

Be creative about who you find to become readers.

- ✦ Retirees, including students' grandparents
- ✦ Students' older brothers or sisters
- ✦ Fraternity or sorority members (They often require service hours.)
- ✦ National Honor Society and Junior National Honor Society members (They also need service hours.)
- ✦ Students who owe community service time because of rule infractions
- ✦ PTA members
- ✦ Students' classmates who finish work early
- ✦ Parents who can record on their lunch hours
- ✦ Business or community partners (They often want to volunteer but don't have big blocks of time.)

✔ Reading aloud and making audiotapes can be time consuming, so don't try to do it alone. Find volunteers. Give each volunteer some blank cassette tapes, lend them a tape recorder if they need one, then give them a passage to read. Include content material from classes as well as story or trade books. Use the Reader Friendly form to organize your readers. Once you have one tape, you can copy it to share with other students.

Reader Friendly

Thanks for volunteering to create a tape for a student. Here are the details:

Please read _____

from page _____ to page _____.

Special instructions: _____

_____

_____

Reader Friendly

Thanks for volunteering to create a tape for a student. Here are the details:

Please read _____

from page _____ to page _____.

Special instructions: _____

_____

_____

Idea 13

Idea 14
Use "Picture This" as a Reminder

All students need help remembering what they are supposed to do. Picture This provides pictures of on- and off-task behaviors and a form students can use to record themselves. You can use the recording form along with the beeper tape described earlier (see Idea 10, page 47) or with a random timer. You can also check students at times when most of them are working hard and on-task. This gives them positive feedback and puts them on the road to success.

Note. This idea was adapted from *Kid Mod: Empowering Children and Youth Through Instruction in the Use of Reinforcement Principles* (p. 345), by J. S. Kaplan with M. G. Kamperman, 1996, Austin, TX: PRO-ED, Inc. Copyright 1996 by PRO-ED, Inc. Adapted with permission.

Picture This

On-Task	Off-Task

	On-Task	Off-Task
1	☐	☐
2	☐	☐
3	☐	☐
4	☐	☐
5	☐	☐
6	☐	☐
7	☐	☐
8	☐	☐
9	☐	☐
10	☐	☐
11	☐	☐
12	☐	☐

Total On-Task = _____

Total Intervals = _____

Percentage On-Task = _____

Idea 14

Idea 15
Teach Students To Raise Their On-Task Awareness

Older students can work with their teachers to rate their own on-task behavior periodically during a class period. After completing a self-rating on the On-Task Awareness form, the student compares his or her rating to the teacher's and receives points for perfect matches. The greatest benefit from this activity is the student's increased awareness of how often he or she is off-task. The purpose of comparing scores with the teacher is to encourage students to develop a realistic picture of their own work behavior. Students should not be discouraged if they fail to match the teacher's evaluation every time. Improvement in on-task behavior is the goal.

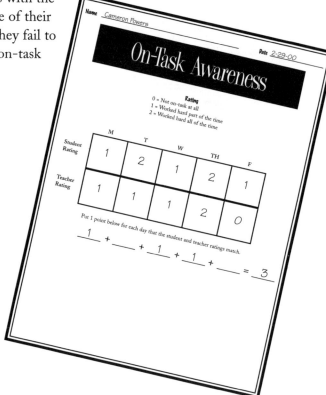

On-Task Awareness

Rating

0 = Not on-task at all
1 = Worked hard part of the time
2 = Worked hard all of the time

	M	T	W	TH	F
Student Rating					
Teacher Rating					

Put 1 point below for each day that the student and teacher ratings match.

_____ + _____ + _____ + _____ + _____ = _____

Idea 15

Idea 16
Use Victim Cards

All students enjoy it when teachers "hype" things up to keep their attention. At the beginning of the school year, have each student print or write his or her name on a Victim Card. After you collect them, laminate the cards and put them together with a rubber band or in a small box so that they make a deck of cards. To keep students' attention, use the victim cards as a way to randomly call on them for answers.

"Let's see now, who's my next victim?"

✔ Shuffle the cards often so students don't quit paying attention after their turn.

My Next Victim Is:

_____

My Next Victim Is:

_____

My Next Victim Is:

_____

My Next Victim Is:

_____

My Next Victim Is:

_____

My Next Victim Is:

_____

My Next Victim Is:

_____

My Next Victim Is:

_____

Idea 16

My Next Victim Is:

_____

My Next Victim Is:

_____

My Next Victim Is:

_____

My Next Victim Is:

_____

My Next Victim Is:

_____

My Next Victim Is:

_____

My Next Victim Is:

_____

My Next Victim Is:

_____

62

Idea 16

Idea 17
Establish Teacher Talk Time

Teacher Talk Time (Triple T) works for **all students**.

Here's what to do.

Before you begin, locate a timer, a large clear plastic tub or jar, and your Yes/No tickets (see forms for this section). The Yes coupons should be copied on bright green paper and the No coupons on bright red paper. When you are ready, follow these steps.

1 First, explain to students that during direct instruction time (Teacher Talk Time), it is important that the teacher does the talking. However, the time will be limited and will not exceed a specified limit.

2 Second, explain the two rules during Triple T:
- Only the teacher talks, unless students are called on by name to answer a question.
- Students must stay seated.

3 Third, set a timer for an appropriate amount of direct instruction time. For young students, try 5–10 minutes. For older students, try 10–20 minutes. If your students are distracted by the ticking timer, buy an inexpensive battery timer or set a watch that has a beeper. Tell your students that you absolutely promise to stop talking when the timer goes off, even if you are not completely finished. (You can always take a short break, then begin another Triple T session.)

4 Fourth, as you lecture, explain, or demonstrate, use the Yes/No tickets to give students visible feedback on how they are doing following the two rules. Every two to three minutes, put a Yes ticket in the jar if students are following the two rules and a No coupon in if someone breaks a rule. Do not interrupt your discussion to reprimand, warn, or remind. Just use the tickets.

5 Finally, after the session, praise students for following the rules. At the end of the class period, day, or week (depending on the age of your students), make a big fuss about reaching into the jar with eyes closed and pulling out a ticket. A No means no reward, but a Yes means the entire class gets a goodie. Consider these options for class rewards:
- Extra recess or conversation time
- A night off from homework
- Extra points on the class participation average
- Snacks or soft drinks during seatwork time (Students can bring their own.)
- A quick game or "read aloud" by the teacher

Note. Part of this idea was adapted from *TGIF: But What Will I Do on Monday?* (p. 23), by S. L. Fister and K. A. Kemp, 1995, Longmont, CO: Sopris West. Copyright 1995 by Susan L. Fister and Karen A. Kemp. Adapted with permission.

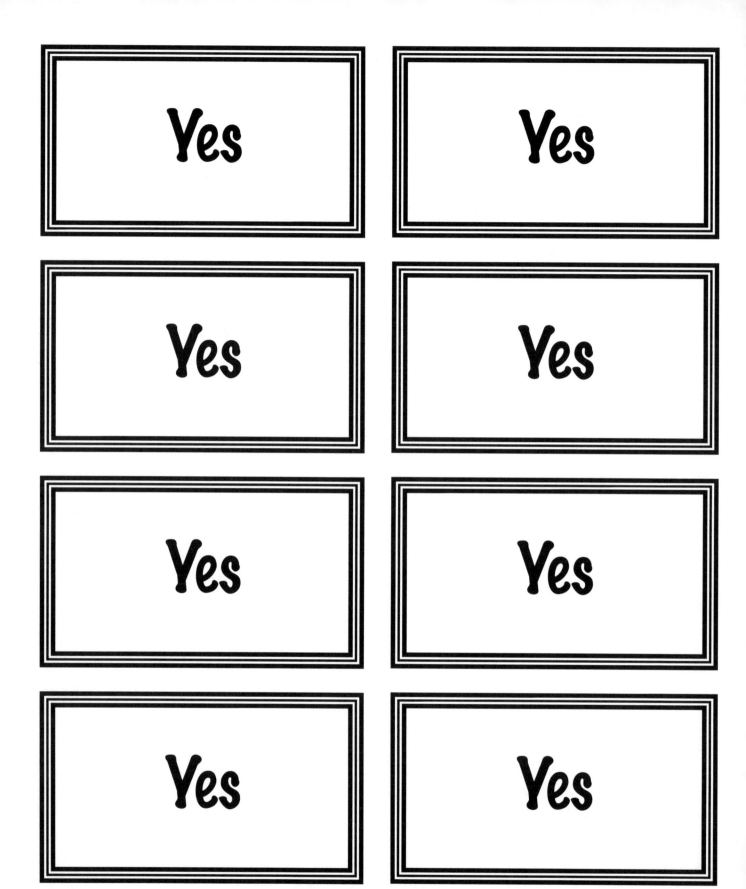

Idea 17

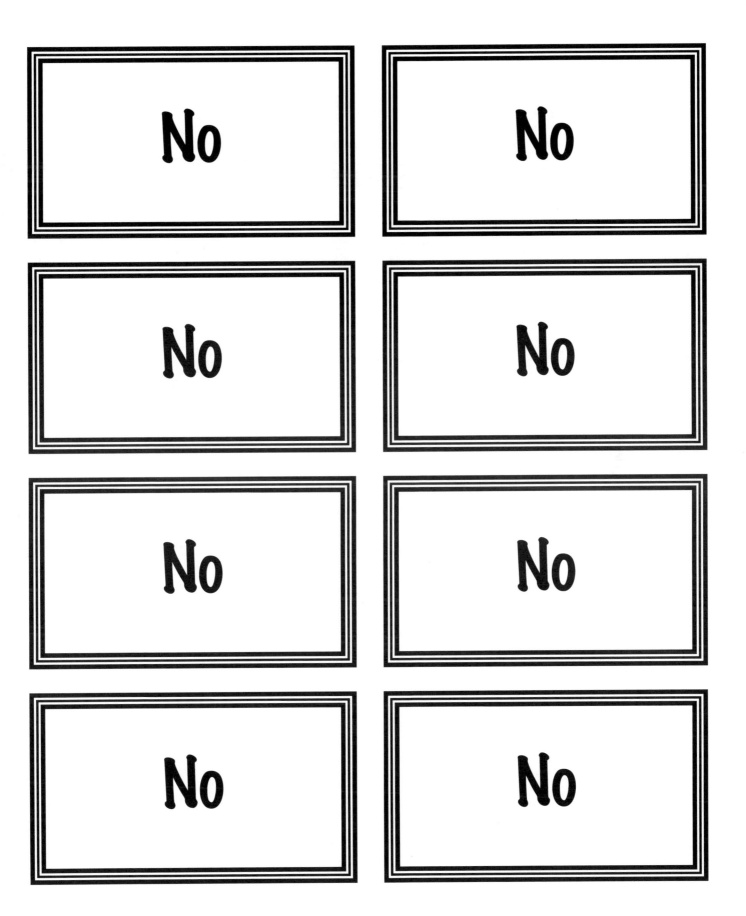

Idea 18
Develop a Two-Way Agreement in the Form of a Contract

All students need support to reach their goals, and students with attention problems are no exception. A two-way agreement in the form of a contract specifies precisely how a student will behave or what task the student will accomplish and in what time frame. It also specifies what support a teacher, parent, administrator, and/or other person will provide in order to assist the student in meeting his or her goals.

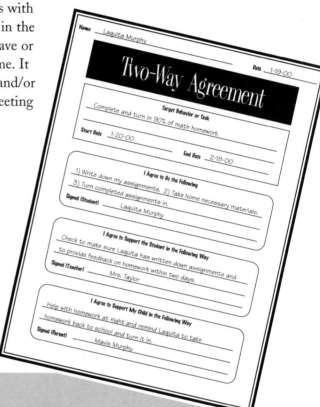

Follow these steps.

1 Meet with the student to discuss the target behavior or task.

2 Collaborate to decide on the specific type of behavior the student will exhibit, the time span of the contract, and the specific support given to the student.

3 Complete the form and have all parties sign.

Two-Way Agreement

Target Behavior or Task

_____

_____

Start Date _____   End Date _____

I Agree to Do the Following

_____

_____

Signed (Student) _____

I Agree to Support the Student in the Following Way

_____

_____

Signed (Teacher) _____

I Agree to Support My Child in the Following Way

_____

_____

Signed (Parent) _____

Idea 19
Teach Students To Be Bragging Buddies

In order to build group cohesiveness and help **all students** see themselves as part of the solution instead of part of the problem in the classroom, teach your students to become Bragging Buddies.

Here's what to do.

1 First, write or print brag phrases on cards. Focus on simple, fun ways students can encourage each other. Set the cards in the middle of the students' tables or desks and post them on the wall so that they are always visible. Start with two basic brags: "Good job" and "Good try."

2 When a student makes a correct statement or gets something right, students say "Good job." If the answer is incorrect, someone still offers a brag: "Good try." After students get the hang of it, gradually add other brags so that they students have lots of choices, but are not overwhelmed.

3 Make sure that all students praise each other. You can do this by passing out tickets at the beginning of the day or class, one per student. After a student praises a peer, he or she puts a ticket in the jar and is qualified for the Bragging Bonus. The Bragging Bonus is randomly selected during by drawing a name, which entitles the student to a pencil, pen, candy bar, ice cream bar at lunchtime, trip to visit the principal, lunch with the teacher, pizza party at the end of two weeks, or other treat.

4 After every student comment, regardless of whether it is correct, students should reinforce each other with a brag. Here are some ideas:

- You go, guy!
- You go, girl!
- Nice try!
- I like it!
- Way to go!
- That's the best!
- You can do it!
- Hot dog!
- You got it!

5 After your students have become good Bragging Buddies, set aside a few minutes each Monday morning to have them decide on the brags for the week.

Bragging Buddy

I am a Bragging Buddy.
Please enter me in the Bragging Bonus drawing.

My name is _____

Bragging Buddy

I am a Bragging Buddy.
Please enter me in the Bragging Bonus drawing.

My name is _____

Bragging Buddy

I am a Bragging Buddy.
Please enter me in the Bragging Bonus drawing.

My name is _____

Bragging Buddy

I am a Bragging Buddy.
Please enter me in the Bragging Bonus drawing.

My name is _____

Bragging Buddy

I am a Bragging Buddy.
Please enter me in the Bragging Bonus drawing.

My name is _____

Bragging Buddy

I am a Bragging Buddy.
Please enter me in the Bragging Bonus drawing.

My name is _____

Bragging Buddy

I am a Bragging Buddy.
Please enter me in the Bragging Bonus drawing.

My name is _____

Bragging Buddy

I am a Bragging Buddy.
Please enter me in the Bragging Bonus drawing.

My name is _____

Idea 19

This week's brag is

Idea 20

Provide Homework Assignment Forms and Checksheets

Getting homework completed and turned in can be a real pain for students, their parents, and their teachers. **All students** can benefit from tools that help them stay organized and on track with homework assignments. Several assignment forms are provided that can be used for students of all ages. Just having the forms is not enough, though. Teachers should teach students how to use them, let parents know what their role is in monitoring homework completion, and then reward students for using the forms regularly.

✔ Parents will really appreciate these organizational tools, especially as their children get older and need to develop more independence.

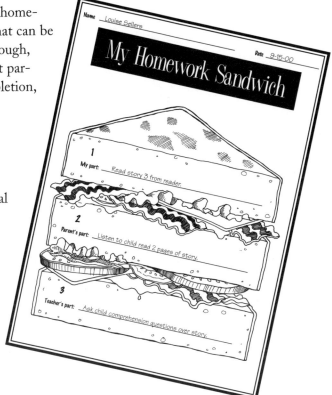

My Homework Sandwich

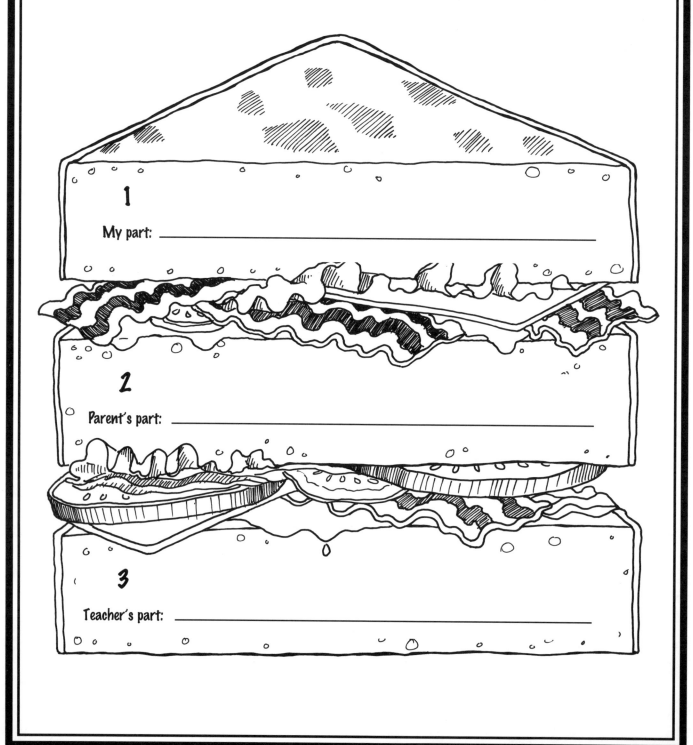

1

My part: _____

2

Parent's part: _____

3

Teacher's part: _____

Idea 20

Home/School Assignments

Subject	Assignments Due Tomorrow	Homework Due Today	Today's Classwork	Initials
_____ _____ _____	_____ _____	☐ Complete ☐ Not complete	☐ Complete ☐ Not complete	Teacher _____ Parent _____
_____ _____ _____	_____ _____	☐ Complete ☐ Not complete	☐ Complete ☐ Not complete	Teacher _____ Parent _____
_____ _____ _____	_____ _____	☐ Complete ☐ Not complete	☐ Complete ☐ Not complete	Teacher _____ Parent _____
_____ _____ _____	_____ _____	☐ Complete ☐ Not complete	☐ Complete ☐ Not complete	Teacher _____ Parent _____
_____ _____ _____	_____ _____	☐ Complete ☐ Not complete	☐ Complete ☐ Not complete	Teacher _____ Parent _____

Idea 20

Homework Assignments

Subject	Assignment	Due Date
_____	_____	_____
_____	_____	_____
_____	_____	_____
_____	_____	_____
_____	_____	_____
_____	_____	_____
_____	_____	_____

Materials Needed

- _____
- _____
- _____
- _____

- _____
- _____
- _____
- _____

Idea 20

Homework Plan

Fill in **What** the assignment is, **When** it is due, and **Who** and **What** you need for help.
☑ Put a check mark in the box after you complete each assignment.

	What	When	Who/What Can Help	When Complete ☑
Monday				☐
Tuesday				☐
Wednesday				☐
Thursday				☐
Friday				☐

Idea 20

Long-Range Assignment Planner

Assignment/Project _____

Due Date _____

PART 1 _____

Due Date _____
Teacher's Initials _____
Student's Initials _____

PART 2 _____

Due Date _____
Teacher's Initials _____
Student's Initials _____

PART 3 _____

Due Date _____
Teacher's Initials _____
Student's Initials _____

PART 4 _____

Due Date _____
Teacher's Initials _____
Student's Initials _____

PART 5 _____

Due Date _____
Teacher's Initials _____
Student's Initials _____

PART 6 _____

Due Date _____
Teacher's Initials _____
Student's Initials _____

Idea 20

Form
Provided

Idea 21
Use a Variety of Questioning Techniques

All students can benefit from these questioning techniques.

1 Begin the question with a student's name.

"Gail, who wrote To Kill a Mockingbird*?"*

❥ This focuses the student's attention *before* you ask the question and keeps him or her "with you."

2 Have students question a partner after you model the type of question.

"Turn to your partner and ask him or her what the steps are in the experiment."

❥ This allows students to get information from each other and teaches them what to ask themselves during a lesson.

3 Alternate individual and group questions.

"Everyone who thinks the answer is 5, hold up your dry erase board. Now, Bill, tell me what you did first.""

❥ Group responses are also quick and don't interupt the flow of the lesson. They are also an effective and efficient method of assessing how much the class is learning from your instruction. For a more complete assessment, combine group responses with individual questioning, which is critical for measuring individual students' progress.

4 Ask both open-ended and specific recall types of questions.

"Which type of boat do you think would work best?," "Why do you think so?," and *"What materials were used to build the boats?"*

❥ Student's with ADHD are often great at getting the big idea but may miss the details. They not only need a chance to shine with open-ended questions but also to practice focusing with more specific questions.

5 Use a ticket or token system to make sure everyone takes a turn answering your questions and no one monopolizes the conversation.

Pass out one ticket to each student. Have the students hand you their ticket as they answer a question. Once a student has answered and has no ticket left, it is someone else's turn to provide a response.

❥ This strategy encourages the talkative student with ADHD to keep a lid on his or her talk-outs and may help the reluctant student to get more actively involved.

Talk Ticket

The bearer of this ticket
is permitted to talk

1 Time

Talk Ticket

The bearer of this ticket
is permitted to talk

1 Time

Talk Ticket

The bearer of this ticket
is permitted to talk

1 Time

Talk Ticket

The bearer of this ticket
is permitted to talk

1 Time

Talk Ticket

The bearer of this ticket
is permitted to talk

1 Time

Talk Ticket

The bearer of this ticket
is permitted to talk

1 Time

Talk Ticket

The bearer of this ticket
is permitted to talk

1 Time

Talk Ticket

The bearer of this ticket
is permitted to talk

1 Time

Talk Ticket

The bearer of this ticket
is permitted to talk

1 Time

Talk Ticket

The bearer of this ticket
is permitted to talk

1 Time

Talk Ticket

The bearer of this ticket
is permitted to talk

1 Time

Talk Ticket

The bearer of this ticket
is permitted to talk

1 Time

Idea 21

Idea 22
Use Visual Contracts

All students can benefit from visual contracts. Visual contracts help students keep track of their progress, and they also encourage them to keep trying. There are endless possibilities to fit the age and interests of all students, including the following:

- Connect the Dots
- Puzzles
- Color the Dots
- Punch cards

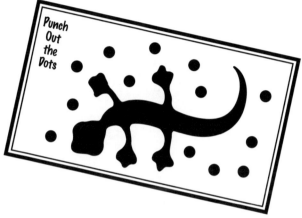

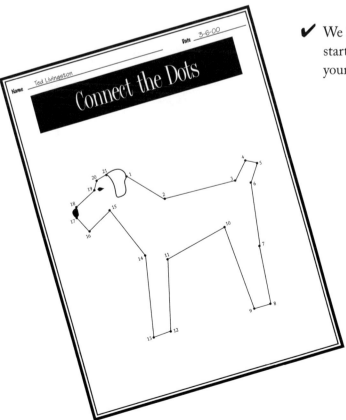

✔ We have provided examples to help you get started, but use your imagination and also let your students help you with ideas.

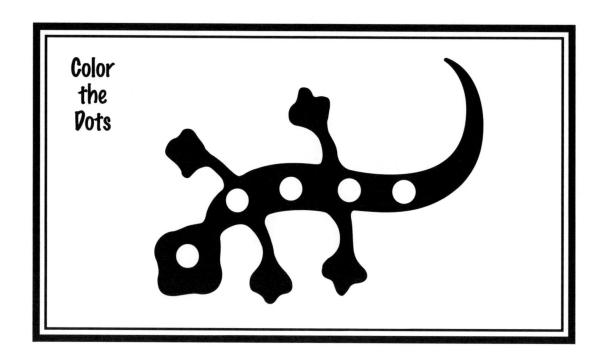

Color
the
Dots

Punch
Out
the
Dots

Idea 22

Connect the Dots

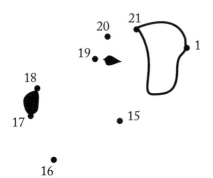

20
21
19
1
18
17
15
16
4
5
2
3
6
10
14
11
7
13   12
9   8

Idea 22

Idea 23
Teach Students To Organize Their Materials

For younger students, use plastic tubs with lids to store distracting materials such as art supplies, rulers, calculators, and so forth. Place the tubs on a shelf and label with each student's name. On the lid of the tub, tape a template or visual checklist that shows the arrangement of the materials in the tub. Review the template or checklist with them each Friday afternoon, so that on Monday morning they are ready to go to work.

Older students will probably need a more portable system, since they often move from room to room when they change subjects. Some ideas to keep middle-grade and secondary students more organized are listed below.

Organization Ideas

1 Have students color code by choosing one color per subject, then making sure that everything related to that subject is the same color. For example, if math is red, then the notebook, folder, and highlighter are all red or pink.

2 Suggest that students buy Post-It flags in each subject color. After assigning homework, direct students to take out a Post-It flag and place it on the assigned page, so that it sticks out and is immediately visible. Even if the book is later piled up in a locker or stuffed into a crowded desk, the student will know that he or she has homework and should take the book out because the flag will be showing.

3 Require students to purchase a calendar and/or organizer. If all students use the same system in all classes, they will be more likely to learn the system and remember to use it.

4 Designate one folder as a "Take Home Folder."

Idea 24
Teach Students To Use Countoons

All students can use countoons. Countoons have been around for many years and have been used successfully by teachers who want quick and easy contracts and monitoring forms for individual students. Countoons are a great tool if you are dealing with a behavior that you want to increase or decrease in frequency.

A countoon is a three-panel cartoon. The first panel shows a picture of what the behavior looks like. Panel two is used for counting the behavior. Panel three is a picture of a reinforcer that will be earned when the student meets an agreed-upon criterion.

Here's what teachers should do.

1 Discuss with the student a problem behavior that needs to change. Set a criterion slightly above or below current performance, depending on whether you would like to reduce or increase the frequency of the behavior. (For example, if Sally is calling out ten times, set her criterion at eight. If Gino is only volunteering in class twice per week, set the criterion at four times per week.)

2 Ask the student to select a reinforcer that he or she would like to earn if the criterion is met.

3 Create the countoon by circling the criterion (e.g., Sally would circle the 8). Duplicate on copy paper or make one sturdy copy on stock paper and laminate.

4 Teach the student to self-record his or her behavior by crossing through consecutive numbers each time he or she demonstrates the behavior. Do a couple of practice sessions in which both the teacher and student monitor, then compare the two recordings.

5 Either place the countoon permanently on the student's desk, or if using regular copies, use one per day or class period.

6 Once the student meets the criterion, immediately provide the reinforcer.

Countoon Contract

What I Do	How Many	What I Get
	1 2 3 4 5 6 7 8 9 10 11 12	

Idea 25

Provide Reminders Before Tests or When Projects Are Due

Teachers often require students to take tests or quizzes home to show their parents. Unfortunately, this process usually occurs *after* a student has failed or has not done well. We suggest that you take a more proactive approach. Provide reminders for students (and their parents) *before* the test.

All students can benefit. Older students will be more likely to respond if you give them extra points on their homework or test averages for returning the form.

✔ Copy the reminders on bright paper that is impossible to miss.

Don't Forget

On _____

☐ It's test time.
☐ It's time to turn in

_____

_____
Parent Signature

Don't Forget

On _____

☐ It's test time.
☐ It's time to turn in

_____

_____
Parent Signature

Don't Forget

On _____

☐ It's test time.
☐ It's time to turn in

_____

_____
Parent Signature

Don't Forget

On _____

☐ It's test time.
☐ It's time to turn in

_____

_____
Parent Signature

Idea 25

It's
TEST TIME
Again

_____
Subject

_____
Date of Test

_____
Student Signature

_____
Parent Signature

Start Getting Ready for Your
Big Date

_____
Test Subject

_____
Date of Test

_____
Student Signature

_____
Parent Signature

It's
TEST TIME
Again

_____
Subject

_____
Date of Test

_____
Student Signature

_____
Parent Signature

Don't Forget Our Date

_on_ _____

for a Test

_in_ _____

_____
Student Signature

_____
Parent Signature

Idea 25

Idea 26
Give Your Students a Structured Format for Spelling and Vocabulary Work

We often expect students to have good study skills without teaching those skills. Unfortunately, many students are at a loss when it comes time to take notes, organize information, and then study. The following two forms should keep things organized and provide a framework for review. These forms are for spelling and vocabulary, but you can easily adapt them for other subjects.

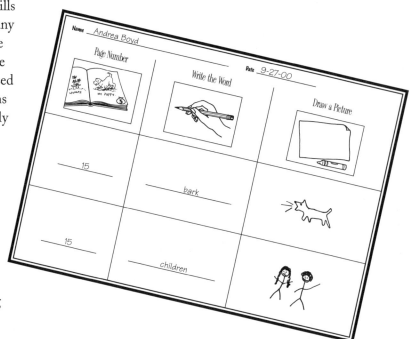

For younger students, use the version with visual cues. Pictures let them know what to do when they cannot read instructions. Using the form will help them learn to organize information while they are still young and should help prepare them for more detailed note taking later.

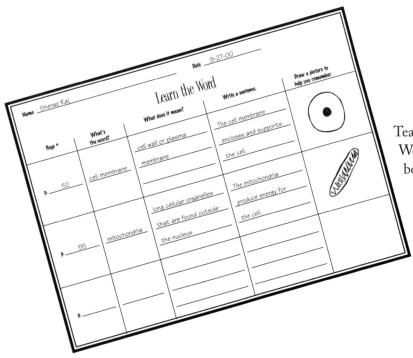

Teach **older students** to use the Learn the Word form, which they can keep in their notebooks for later review and test preparation.

Name _____ Date _____

Page Number

Write the Word

Draw a Picture

_____ _____

_____ _____

Name _____   Date _____

Learn the Word

Page #	What's the word?	What does it mean?	Write a sentence.	Draw a picture to help you remember.
p. _____	_____	_____ _____ _____	_____ _____ _____	
p. _____	_____	_____ _____ _____	_____ _____ _____	
p. _____	_____	_____ _____ _____	_____ _____ _____	

Idea 27
Let Students Leave, But Make It Worthwhile To Stay

Older students love to leave class to go to lockers, get a drink of water, or go to the restroom. When students get up and leave or ask to leave only occasionally, it does not disrupt instruction and is no problem. However, when students constantly ask to leave the room, it becomes a problem.

One solution is for you to allow them a certain number of "free" hall passes, such as our *Get Out of Class Free* cards. We suggest giving each student two cards per six weeks. Distribute them the first day of each new marking period after writing the students' names on them in ink. (Or you can have them do it themselves.) When a student wants to leave the room for some reason, he hands over a card. Only two trips are allowed each marking period. However, for each card not used, the student can add points to his or her grade or test average, or drop a homework grade.

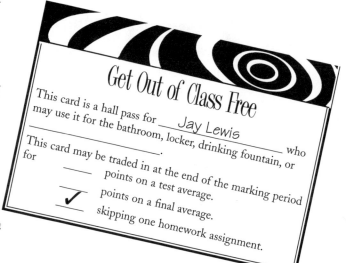

Get Out of Class Free

This card is a hall pass for _____ who may use it for the bathroom, locker, drinking fountain, or _____.

This card may be traded in at the end of the marking period for _____ points on a test average.

_____ points on a final average.

_____ skipping one homework assignment.

Get Out of Class Free

This card is a hall pass for _____ who may use it for the bathroom, locker, drinking fountain, or _____.

This card may be traded in at the end of the marking period for _____ points on a test average.

_____ points on a final average.

_____ skipping one homework assignment.

Get Out of Class Free

This card is a hall pass for _____ who may use it for the bathroom, locker, drinking fountain, or _____.

This card may be traded in at the end of the marking period for _____ points on a test average.

_____ points on a final average.

_____ skipping one homework assignment.

Get Out of Class Free

This card is a hall pass for _____ who may use it for the bathroom, locker, drinking fountain, or _____.

This card may be traded in at the end of the marking period for _____ points on a test average.

_____ points on a final average.

_____ skipping one homework assignment.

Get Out of Class Free

This card is a hall pass for _____ who may use it for the bathroom, locker, drinking fountain, or _____.

This card may be traded in at the end of the marking period for _____ points on a test average.

_____ points on a final average.

_____ skipping one homework assignment.

Get Out of Class Free

This card is a hall pass for _____ who may use it for the bathroom, locker, drinking fountain, or _____.

This card may be traded in at the end of the marking period for _____ points on a test average.

_____ points on a final average.

_____ skipping one homework assignment.

Idea 27

Form Provided

Idea 28
Use Peers To Double-Check and Edit

Students in Grades 4 and higher can team up to check and offer help to each other. This strategy can be a big timesaver for teachers. Distribute the Team Checker cards to students each morning and start the day with a peer check. Students check each other again at the end of the day. Older students can also follow up with a reminder telephone call in the evening. Students who complete their cards can put them in a big jar for a raffle that's held each Friday. The winning team can be rewarded with a No Homework Pass or a special lunch for two.

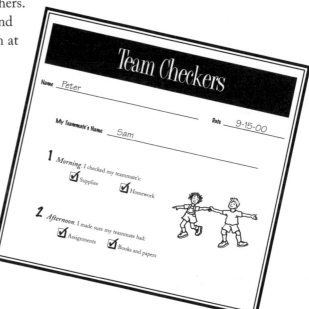

younger students

Team Checkers

Name Peter

My Teammate's Name   Sam   Date 9-15-00

1 *Morning.* I checked my teammate's:
- ☑ Supplies   ☑ Homework

2 *Afternoon.* I made sure my teammate had:
- ☑ Assignments   ☑ Books and papers

older students

Team Checkers

Date 8-23-00

Name Sherrie Wilson

My Teammate's Name   Demitra
My Teammate's Telephone Number   326-9012

1 *In the morning,* I checked to make sure my teammate:
- ☐ Had his or her supplies
- ☑ Brought his or her homework

2 *In the afternoon,* I checked to make sure my teammate:
- ☑ Wrote down the assignments
- ☑ Had the books/papers needed

3 *In the evening,* I called my teammate to:
- ☑ Offer my help
- ☐ Remind him or her to do homework

✔ Switch partners frequently so that students get to know everyone in the class.

Team Checkers

Name _____ Date _____

My Teammate's Name _____

1 **Morning**. I checked my teammate's:

☐ Supplies   ☐ Homework

2 **Afternoon**. I made sure my teammate had:

☐ Assignments   ☐ Books and papers

Idea 28

Team Checkers

Name _____ Date _____

My Teammate's Name _____

My Teammate's Telephone Number _____

1 **In the morning,** I checked to make sure my teammate:

   ❑ Had his or her supplies

   ❑ Brought his or her homework

2 **In the afternoon,** I checked to make sure my teammate:

   ❑ Wrote down the assignments

   ❑ Had the books/papers needed

3 **In the evening,** I called my teammate to:

   ❑ Offer my help

   ❑ Remind him or her to do homework

Idea 28

Idea 29
Teach Relaxation Techniques

Many students who seem always "on the go" need some strategies to help slow down. Below are some techniques that you can teach students to help them learn to relax. (After you teach the techniques, play soft background music.) You may want to use these techniques at set times of the day with the whole class or with individual students using a cueing system.

Some Relaxation Techniques

1 Breathe in through your nose, counting slowly from 1 to 5; hold your breath counting to 5 again; now, breathe out through your mouth, counting to 5.

2 Focus all your attention at the tip of your nose. In your mind, watch the breath flowing in and out. Count from 1 to 10 each time you breathe in and out.

3 Visualize yourself stepping onto the top of an escalator. As you breathe slowly in and out, watch yourself descend into a deeper state of relaxation.

4 Think of a peaceful place where you usually feel relaxed and happy, such as the park, the lake, or a favorite vacation spot. Picture yourself there, remembering all of the sights, smells, and tastes you experienced while there. Try to maintain a sense of well-being.

Repeat each technique for at least 3 to 5 minutes
or until the student(s) feels completely relaxed.

Idea 30
Teach Visualization Techniques

All students who have difficulty focusing need strategies to help them "tune in." Visualization can help students "talk" to their subconscious about what they want to achieve or what results they want.

Some Visualization Techniques

1 Relax deeply using one of the relaxation techniques in Idea 29. Focus on a goal you would like to achieve. Picture yourself achieving the goal, including all the people involved in helping you reach the goal. Focus on positive feelings.

2 Focus on a presentation you may be about to give. See yourself presenting your information in a clear, interesting way. See your audience understanding you. Focus on positive feelings.

3 Focus on a problem situation. What do you want your end results to be? How do you want it to be resolved? Picture that happening with as much detail as possible. Bring all your senses into play. Picture positive interactions between you and the other person(s) involved.

Idea 31
Create a Quiet Corner

All students can become fidgety and squirmy, but for those who consistently move a lot, create a special place where distractions are few and any disruptions are less likely to be seen or heard by other students.

✔ By careful observation and questioning, teachers may be able to determine which environmental conditions are best for individual students.

Some ideas to make your quiet corner more effective.

1 Keep the quiet corner away from traffic to and from the pencil sharpener, doorway, teacher's desk, bathroom, and water fountain.

2 Make the quiet corner a soothing (not a punishing) place. Do not use the quiet corner as a negative consequence or for punishment time-outs.

3 Remove posters and other distracting signs. Include some green plants. If you can paint, use a soothing, calm color on the walls.

4 For students who need formal furniture, use a study carrel that has sides and plenty of flat writing space. For students who need a more relaxed setting in which to calm down, use big pillows or a beanbag chair.

5 Identify the area with a sign like the one provided.

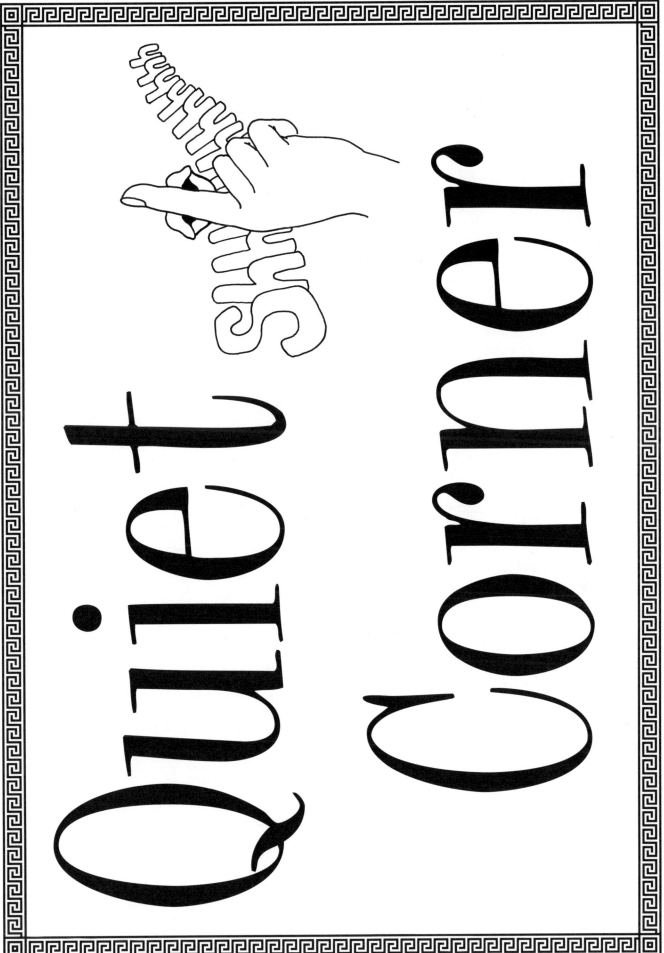

Quiet Corner

Idea 32
Provide Opportunities To Get Physical

Some students have difficulty sitting still, and some have an abundance of nervous energy and actually learn better when moving about. During a lesson, a video, or discussion, it is sometimes helpful to provide opportunities for these students to channel their energy.

Some Ideas

1 If there are animals or plants in the room, have the student feed the animals, clean the fish tank, or water the plants.

2 For a student who likes to clean, have him or her dust the furniture, straighten and clean the bookshelf, clean the chalkboard, or wash the windows.

3 For a student who just cannot sit for long periods of time, allow him or her to move to a designated place at the back of the room and stand.

4 Occasionally let the student run an errand or deliver something to the office or another classroom.

Idea 33

Use a Structured Visual Warning System Along with a Behavior Book

For students in the intermediate grades, this two-part strategy works very well. The first part of the system is a structured visual warning system. If a student is disruptive during instruction, the teacher walks to the student's desk and places a bright yellow yield sign on it. If the disruption continues, the red stop sign is used next. Both are placed on the desk without discussion and without interrupting instruction. When the lesson is over, the student is required to write in the behavior book why the signs were given. After a predetermined number of infractions are recorded in the book, the system of consequences is implemented, including perhaps a student–teacher–parent conference or a loss of privileges. Since the strategy is used without discussion, it must be explained and modeled several times *before* it is used, giving students a chance to practice their responses.

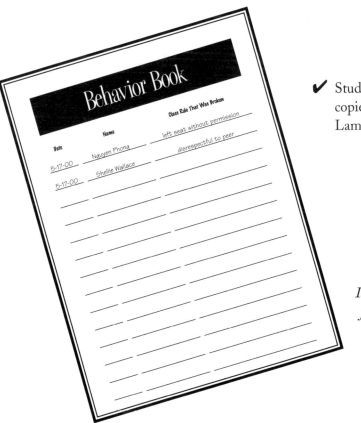

✔ Students will attend to these signs better if the yield is copied on bright yellow paper and the stop sign on red. Laminate both so they can be used several times.

Idea provided by and used with permission of Kim Hill, fourth-grade teacher, Pine Tree Intermediate School, Longview, Texas.

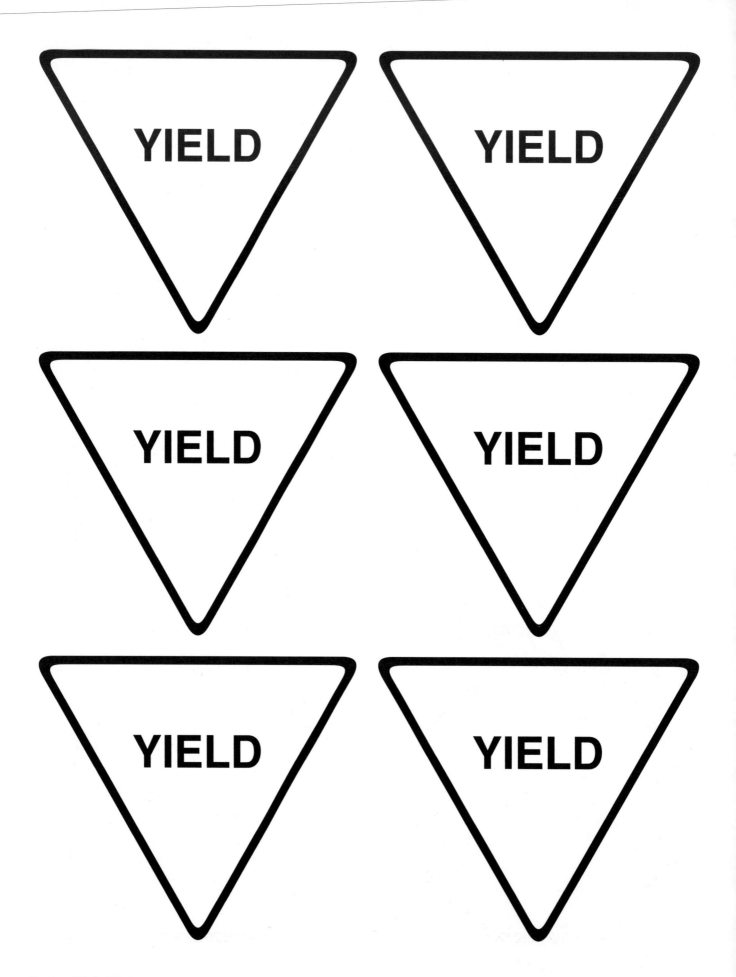

102

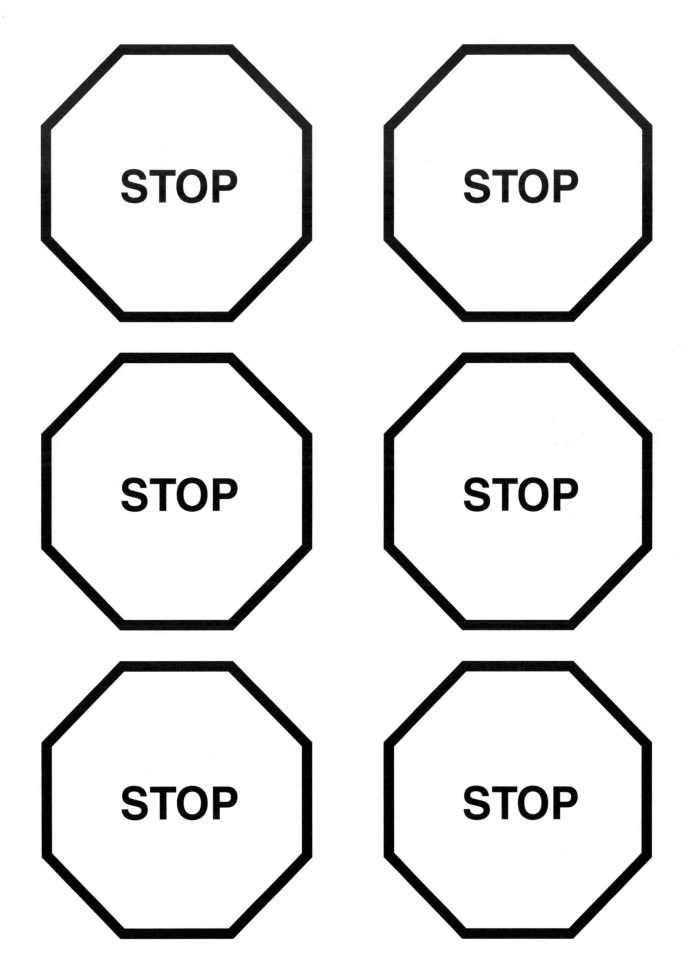

103

Idea 33

Behavior Book

Date	Name	Class Rule That Was Broken
_____	_____	_____
_____	_____	_____
_____	_____	_____
_____	_____	_____
_____	_____	_____
_____	_____	_____
_____	_____	_____
_____	_____	_____
_____	_____	_____
_____	_____	_____
_____	_____	_____
_____	_____	_____
_____	_____	_____

Idea 33

Idea 34
Modify Distracters and Habitual Activities

All students can learn ways to keep their tapping, rapping, tugging, humming, twitching, flapping, snapping, bobbing, and rocking quiet.

Some Ideas

1 For students who tap, give them a mouse pad or some soft, thick shelf paper to use instead of their desktop.

2 For students who need to use their hands, provide a soft squeeze ball.

3 For a student who likes to stand and move about, use colored electrical tape to create a boundary around his or her desk. Allow enough room to get up and move, but not enough space to bother other students.

4 When you have a student who often finishes work early and needs to unwind, provide a Nerf basketball and small hoop that attaches to a trash can or wall. Place the hoop at the back of the classroom, and let the student earn five minutes of basketball time by correctly completing assignments.

Idea 35
Teach Students the "Three Bs"

Teachers frequently find themselves wishing that students with ADHD would demonstrate self-control, especially when interacting with others around them. Actually teaching the self-control skills can be a challenge, however, since teachers have little time and few materials to provide them with ideas. Fortunately, there are some simple ways to teach self-control skills to students that require few materials at all. One example is the *Three Bs*. This is a cognitive-behavioral strategy. Teachers can teach a sequence in which students talk themselves through a situation without losing control.

✔ Students can carry the small, wallet-size reminder card so that they can practice repeating the *Three Bs* throughout the day.

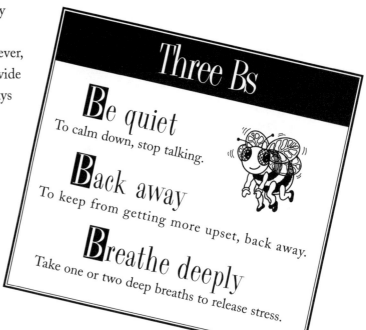

Three Bs

Be quiet
To calm down, stop talking.

Back away
To keep from getting more upset, back away.

Breathe deeply
Take one or two deep breaths to release stress.

How to Teach the "Three Bs"

1 Model for students by saying the steps aloud.

2 Ask students to practice saying the steps aloud.

3 Have students demonstrate the steps without actually talking.

4 Set up scenarios or simulations, and ask students to demonstrate what they would do and how they would react.

5 Provide students with corrective feedback and praise.

Three Bs

Be quiet
To calm down, stop talking.

Back away
To keep from getting more upset, back away.

Breathe deeply
Take one or two deep breaths to release stress.

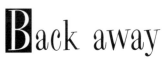

Three Bs

Be quiet
Back away
Breathe deeply

Three Bs

Be quiet
Back away
Breathe deeply

Three Bs

Be quiet
Back away
Breathe deeply

Three Bs

Be quiet
Back away
Breathe deeply

Idea 35

Idea 36
Audiotape the Class During Quiet Seatwork Time

For younger students, set up a cassette recorder and audiotape a short segment of a quiet lesson (e.g., seatwork/independent practice time). About 5 minutes of quiet time for younger students and 15 minutes for older students would be good starting points. After the lesson ends, play back the tape for the class and let students rate their noise level on the forms provided. If you keep hearing just one student all the time, make an individual contract with him or her. Then reward the student if you don't hear him or her during the next taping session.

✔ A sample contract for quiet work is also provided.

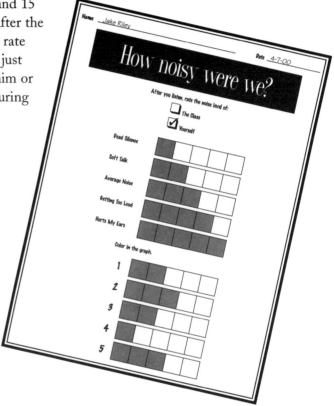

How noisy were we?

After you listen, rate the noise level of:

☐ The Class

☐ Yourself

Dead Silence

Soft Talk

Average Noise

Getting Too Loud

Hurts My Ears

Color in the graph.

1

2

3

4

5

Idea 36

Quiet Is the Key

Each time you make it through a class without bothering anyone, shade in a key on the key ring.
When all of the keys are shaded, you will have earned

_____

Idea 37

Teach Students To Use a Nonverbal Signal System

Younger students can use large signal cards that are attached to the front of their desks. The green side of the card can have a message that indicates that the student is working and does not need assistance. The flip side of the card, copied on red paper, can say "I need help." Either tape the cards to the front of students' desks so that they can flip them up when needed, or use Velcro to fasten the cards to the top corner of the desk.

I'm working hard.

✔ For students who need larger or more visible signals, use two plastic coated paper cups, one red and the other green. Glue or tape them together so that the bottoms of the cups are touching. Students can set them with the green side up when all is going well and the red side up when they need assistance.

Older students can use signals, too, but the signals should be less obvious and more age-appropriate. Both the student and the teacher can use smaller cards to communicate back and forth. Laminate the cards, put them on a key ring or plastic bracelet, and teach students to hold up a card when they have a question or need help. Then, use the teacher's set to signal back to students, letting them know that you have seen them and will get to them as soon as possible.

I'm working hard.

Can you help me?

I'm working hard.

Can you
help me?

⭐ ?

⭐ **ASAP**

⭐ **SOS**

⭐ In a Minute

⭐ I Need Help

⭐ Need Help?

⭐

⭐

Idea 37

Idea 38
Use a Point-and-Clap Routine During Direct Instruction

All students enjoy activities that are fun and different. Routines that involve clapping, snapping, chanting, and/or repetitive phrases can also be used as signals. Point-and-clap combines a visual strategy with an auditory one. When working with students who have attention problems, it is important to use lots of visuals anyway. An overhead projector, white board, and chalkboard are great tools.

Keep students "with you" by using a pointer, ruler, or small flashlight.

1 Point at words, phrases, or problems.

2 As you point, say the word or phrase.

3 Signal with a clap, and repeat the word or phrase again, this time with students joining in the chant.

4 Once the rhythm is established, you can add cues such as, "I say _____. Now you say _____."

5 Consider adding sounds or music that includes repetition and rhythm.

Idea 39
Use Simple Behavior Monitoring Forms

Students with ADHD often benefit from feedback regarding their behavior, as well as positive reinforcement when that behavior is positive and appropriate. Behavior monitoring forms (also called daily report cards) help students maintain their good patterns of behavior. The forms also help teachers respond to those behaviors with consistent positive reinforcement. Each time students do well, the teacher has an opportunity to praise and reward. Three behavior monitoring forms are provided, two for young students and one for older students.

For younger students, use a behavior monitoring form that is simple, clear, and does not require high-level reading skills.

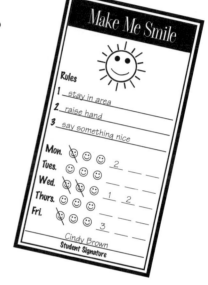

✔ To improve school–home communication, the forms should also be easy for parents to understand.

Older students should have a monitoring form that follows them from class to class. In both cases, it is important that the form is quick and easy to complete, or other teachers will not use it.

Directions for Forms

Make Me Smile

Write three simple rules (e.g., stay in area; raise hand; say something nice). If a rule is broken, cross off a smiley face and write the rule number in the blank to the side. If at least one smiley face is left each day, the student earns points or tickets.

Super-duper Behavior

Each activity to be rated is depicted by a picture to provide the student with a visual cue. Each picture corresponds to a box next to the day of the week. A fun sticker is placed in the corresponding box when the student follows the class rules. The student can earn bonus points for exceptional behavior, or rewards if a predetermined number of stickers is earned each day or during the week. This chart can be sent home for parental review.

Daily Tracking Form

This form tracks three specific behaviors and rates overall behavior for a student throughout a school day or in selected classes. The teacher checks the appropriate box to indicate if the student was on time to class, prepared for class, and if homework was assigned. Additionally, the student's behavior is rated as excellent, fair, or poor by using the key at the bottom of the chart. The teacher signs or initials the last box. This form should go home on a daily basis so that the parent can provide a reinforcer for appropriate behavior.

Note. The Make Me Smile idea provided by and used with permission of Angela Burns, third-grade teacher, Pine Tree Intermediate School, Longview, Texas. The Daily Tracking Form was adapted from *The Tough Kid Tool Box* (pp. 93 and 111), by W. R. Jenson, G. Rhode, and H. K. Reavis, 1994–1995, Longmont, CO: Sopris West. Copyright 1994–1995 by William R. Jenson, Ginger Rhode, and H. Kenton Reavis. Adapted with permission.

Make Me Smile

Rules

1 _____

2 _____

3 _____

Mon.   ☺ ☺ ☺   ___ ___ ___

Tues. ☺ ☺ ☺   ___ ___ ___

Wed.   ☺ ☺ ☺   ___ ___ ___

Thurs. ☺ ☺ ☺   ___ ___ ___

Fri.   ☺ ☺ ☺   ___ ___ ___

Student Signature

Make Me Smile

Rules

1 _____

2 _____

3 _____

Mon.   ☺ ☺ ☺   ___ ___ ___

Tues. ☺ ☺ ☺   ___ ___ ___

Wed.   ☺ ☺ ☺   ___ ___ ___

Thurs. ☺ ☺ ☺   ___ ___ ___

Fri.   ☺ ☺ ☺   ___ ___ ___

Student Signature

Name _____   Date _____

Super-duper Behavior

<table>
<tr><td>

Ready to Work

</td><td>

Math

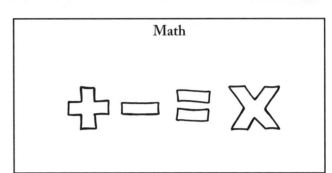

</td></tr>
<tr><td>

Reading

</td><td>

Seatwork

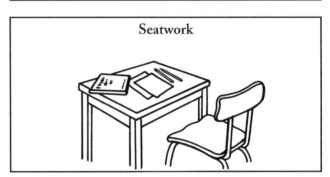

</td></tr>
</table>

Day	Ready to Work	Reading	Math	Seatwork
Monday				
Tuesday				
Wednesday				
Thursday				
Friday				
Bonus Stickers for Extra Super-duper Behavior				

Idea 39

Name _____

Date _____

Daily Tracking Form

Class	On Time?		Prepared?		Homework Assigned?		Behavior			Teacher's Initials
	Yes	No	Yes	No	Yes	No	Excellent	Fair	Poor	
	☐	☐	☐	☐	☐	☐	☐	☐	☐	
	☐	☐	☐	☐	☐	☐	☐	☐	☐	
	☐	☐	☐	☐	☐	☐	☐	☐	☐	
	☐	☐	☐	☐	☐	☐	☐	☐	☐	
	☐	☐	☐	☐	☐	☐	☐	☐	☐	

Key for Behavior:

Excellent
1. Consistently follows classroom rules.
2. Actively listens.
3. Volunteers in class discussions/activities.
4. Speaks respectfully to others.

Fair
1. Follows classroom rules most of the time.
2. Listens at least 75% of the time.
3. Participates when called upon.
4. Speaks respectfully to others some of the time.

Poor
1. Does not follow classroom rules.
2. Does not listen to the teacher.
3. Does not participate in classroom discussions/activities.
4. Is not respectful to others.

Idea 39

Idea 40
Use Positive Reinforcement

The term *positive reinforcement* means a consequence that increases a behavior. Teachers who use positive reinforcement effectively often see great improvement in students' behavior. Here are some simple ways of making your reinforcement work better.

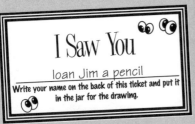

The Reinforcement Menu for Today

- Clean off the overheads
- Wipe the board
- ✓ Run errands today
- Go to lunch 5 minutes early
- Have lunch with your favorite teacher
- Water the plants
- Skip an assignment
- Do half of an assignment
- ✓ A good note to take home
- Talk time with friends
- Empty the trash cans
- Ice cream treat or soda at the end of the day
- Read aloud time for the whole class
- Extra recess or break time for the whole class
- Read a book or magazine alone
- Go to the library
- Grab something from the grab bag
- Take care of the class pets
- Visit another classroom
- Work with a partner instead of alone
- ✓ Extra computer time
- You pick your pen (colored ink, pencil, marker)

A Few Guidelines

1 **Be specific about the behavior you want.** Pick one behavior at a time and specify an action verb. For example:
- *Raise* your hand before talking.
- *Ask* for help when you don't understand.
- *Stay* quiet for at least five minutes.

2 **Be specific about what you say.** Use praise statements that describe the behavior you want. For example:
- Thanks for *waiting so quietly*.
- Great job *getting started so quickly*.

It's still okay to make more general statements like "Super" or "Good work," but more specific verbal statements help students with ADHD to keep focused on the most important behavior.

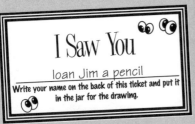

I Saw You

loan Jim a pencil

Write your name on the back of this ticket and put it in the jar for the drawing.

3 **Create a menu of reinforcers and change the menu often.** We have provided an example of a menu as well as a blank menu form so that you can create your own.
- ✔ If you copy the menu on heavy paper and laminate it, you can change the menu daily or weekly by checking off different boxes.

4 **Make sure you (and anyone else working with the student) reinforce consistently.** It is very important that you keep using positive reinforcement even after the student's behavior begins to improve. One way to do this is to begin the class or day with a predetermined number of I Saw You tickets in your pocket. Hand them out each time you notice and praise the student's good behavior. This will ensure that you are consistent with *your* behavior, just as you want your student to be consistent with his or her behavior. When the next class period or day begins, fill your pocket again and start over. Students can put earned tickets in your raffle jar for a later drawing or "spend" them in your class store.

The Reinforcement Menu for Today

- ☐ Clean off the overheads
- ☐ Wipe the board
- ☐ Run errands today
- ☐ Go to lunch 5 minutes early
- ☐ Have lunch with your favorite teacher
- ☐ Water the plants
- ☐ Skip an assignment
- ☐ Do half of an assignment
- ☐ A good note to take home
- ☐ Talk time with friends
- ☐ Empty the trash cans
- ☐ Ice cream treat or soda at the end of the day
- ☐ Read aloud time for the whole class
- ☐ Extra recess or break time for the whole class
- ☐ Read a book or magazine alone
- ☐ Go to the library
- ☐ Grab something from the grab bag
- ☐ Take care of the class pets
- ☐ Visit another classroom
- ☐ Work with a partner instead of alone
- ☐ Extra computer time
- ☐ You pick your pen (colored ink, pencil, marker)

The Reinforcement Menu for Today

- [ ] _____
- [ ] _____
- [ ] _____
- [ ] _____
- [ ] _____
- [ ] _____
- [ ] _____
- [ ] _____
- [ ] _____
- [ ] _____
- [ ] _____
- [ ] _____

Idea 40

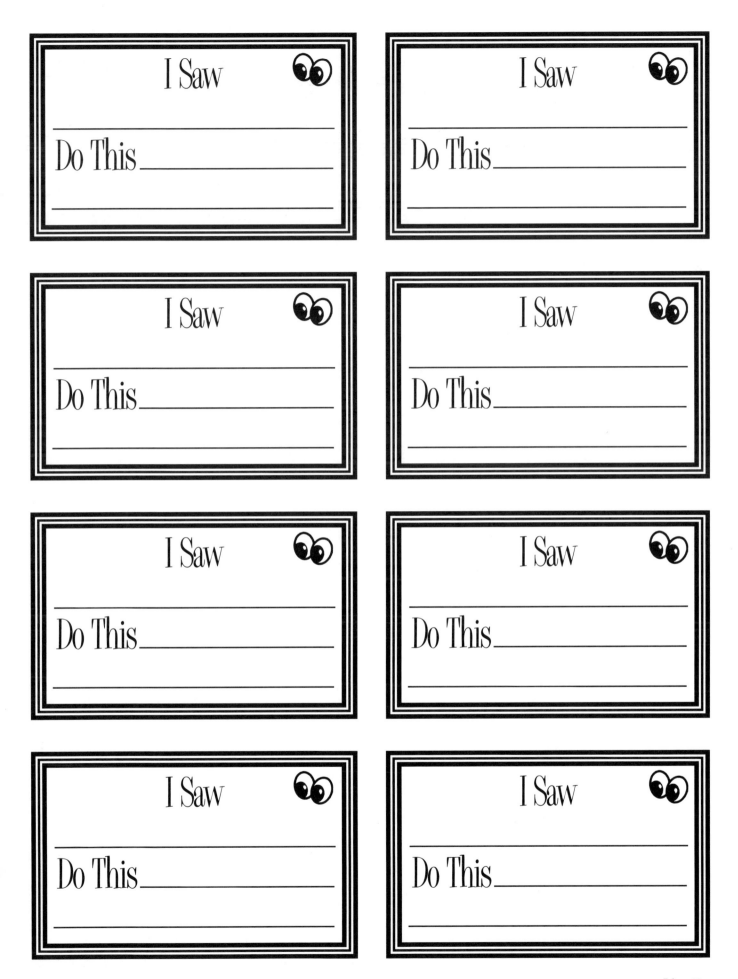

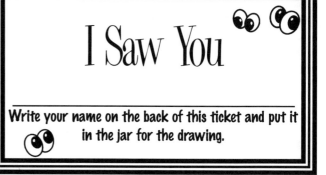

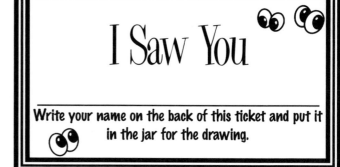

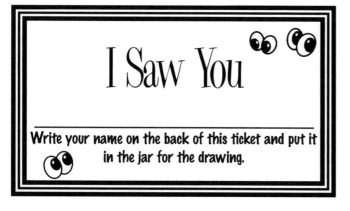

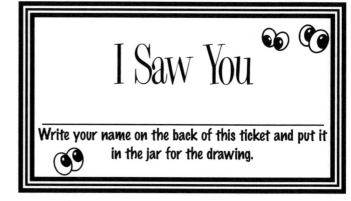

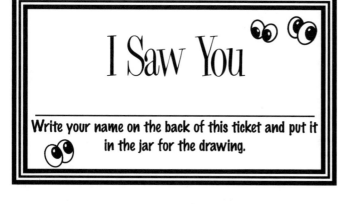

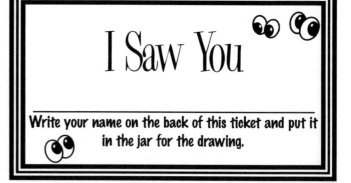

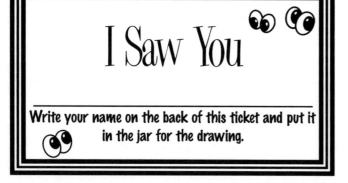

Idea 40

Notes

Notes

Notes

Notes